W9-CEB-989

HOME GROWN GARDENING

CONTAINER AND FRAGRANT GARDENS

HOME GROWN GARDENING

CONTAINER AND FRAGRANT GARDENS

HOW TO ENLIVEN SPACES WITH CONTAINERS AND MAKE THE MOST OF SCENTED PLANTS

PETER LOEWER AND CONTRIBUTORS

Houghton Mifflin Harcourt
BOSTON NEW YORK 2020

Derived from *Taylor's Weekend Gardening Guide to Fragrant Gardens* by Peter Loewer and *Taylor's Guide to Container Gardening*

hmhbooks.com

LIBRARY OF CONGRESS CATALOGING-IN-PUBLICATION DATA

Names: Loewer, H. Peter, author.
Title: Container and fragrant gardens / Peter Loewer.
Description: Boston ; New York : Houghton Mifflin Harcourt, 2020. | Series: Home grown gardening | Includes index.
Identifiers: LCCN 2019009827 (print) | LCCN 2019015387 (ebook) | ISBN 9780358162124 (ebook) | ISBN 9780358161516 (trade paper)
Subjects: LCSH: Container gardening. | Fragrant gardens.
Classification: LCC SB418 (ebook) | LCC SB418 .L62 2020 (print) | DDC 635.9/86—dc23
LC record available at https://lccn.loc.gov/2019009827

ISBN 978-0-358-16151-6

Printed in China

SCP 10 9 8 7 6 5 4 3 2 1

CONTENTS

CONTAINER GARDENS

FRAGRANT GARDENS

HOME GROWN GARDENING

CONTAINER AND FRAGRANT GARDENS

CONTAINER
GARDENS

INTRODUCTION TO CONTAINER GARDENS

Almost everyone can grow plants in containers. Potted gardens grace homes in every region of the country, from the deserts of New Mexico to the forests of Maine, from the mild climes of coastal southern California to the extreme climates of the Great Plains. They're as enjoyable for the owner of an acreage in the country as they are for the city gardener whose "land" extends no farther than the edge of the roof or the ledge of the kitchen window.

With ingenuity and imagination, it is possible to enliven every one of your outdoor living spaces with plants in containers. They can line walkways and balconies, decorate decks and patios, and greet visitors at the door. Hung on fences or under windows, flanking a secluded bench, or mingling with in-ground plantings, in sunny spots or shady, plants in containers add color, fragrance, and eye-catching enjoyment to your property.

Container gardening also expands your gardening options beyond the confines of your site and climate. Because you can maintain tight control of certain conditions—soil, water, nutrients, and exposure—within a pot, container gardening makes accessible a range of plants that would otherwise be difficult or impossible to grow in your garden. And treating a single pot or a group of pots as a miniature garden allows you to experiment with more styles and combinations than you might have space or energy to attempt in a full-scale garden. With a little know-how, patience, and practice, you can grow what you fancy, be it a collection of culinary herbs, continuously blooming annuals, tender tropicals, tiny trees and shrubs, or tasty fruits and vegetables.

pots and planters

PEOPLE GROW PLANTS SUCCESSFULLY IN ALMOST ANY KIND OF CONTAINER, from traditional terra cotta to old toilet bowls. Aside from minimal practical requirements, candidates for containers are limited only by your taste and imagination.

Drainage and size are the prime practical considerations. For all but bog plants, overly moist soil can spell disaster. Drainage holes of some kind in the container are therefore essential. Pot size has an effect on plant health in somewhat more complicated ways. An undersize pot can crowd roots, affecting the plant's supply of water (too much or too little) and nutrients, leading to stifled growth and increased susceptibility to disease. A container that is too big holds extra soil that the plant's roots will be slow to penetrate. This soil will stay wet, and roots in an overly soggy pot begin to rot. The root systems of plants sold at nurseries or garden centers often come close to filling their plastic pots. A good rule of thumb for purchased plants grown for summer display is to select a pot about 2 inches wider and deeper than the one the plant is sold in.

In a hanging basket, a variety of annuals and perennials fill a wire framework.

Clay flue tiles, which come in a range of sizes, can be striking containers.

TERRA COTTA

The pot of choice for more than a century has been one made of clay. Terra cotta (Italian for "baked earth") is valued for more than sentiment and its good looks. Fired clay is porous, allowing air from outside to penetrate and supply oxygen to plant roots. At the same time, excess moisture inside the pot evaporates through the wall. Terra cotta readily absorbs and conducts heat, so high daytime temperatures can cause excessive evaporation and raise soil temperatures to unhealthy levels—in spring, however, the clay will keep the roots of plants somewhat warmer, allowing for a slight jump on the season. Small pots are particularly susceptible to too much evaporation; the greater mass of soil inside larger pots mitigates the effects of heat absorption. Regardless of size, terra-cotta pots in hot, sunny, or windy spots need special attention to watering.

Used thoughtfully, inexpensive plastic pots can look just as good as their pricier cousins.

PLASTIC

Often designed to mimic terra cotta, plastic pots also come in a wide range of sizes, shapes, and colors. They are inexpensive and lightweight. Because their walls aren't porous, soil in them retains moisture longer, which is an advantage for many container plants but not for those, such as herbs or succulents, that prefer drier conditions. The color of the pot is a factor in how much heat it will absorb—soil in lighter-colored pots will remain cooler than soil in dark pots. Plastic pots are less likely to fracture when overwintered outdoors.

CAST CONCRETE

Pots made from cast concrete are very popular because of their good looks. Cast-concrete urns add charm flanking porch steps, especially of Victorian-style homes. Large cast-concrete pots or troughs hold plenty of soil, making extravagant annual displays possible. Many will last for years outside, although their thick walls can still be damaged by the expansion of moist soil as it freezes. Concrete heats up in the sun, like clay, but not quite as quickly, and the larger size of most cast-concrete containers helps moderate overheating.

METAL

Containers of brass, copper, iron, aluminum, or lead are highly ornamental. All make lovely focal points when planted with cascading annual flowers. To protect containers made of ferrous metals from rust, their interiors may be coated with pitch, paint, or wax, which must be reapplied every few years. The thicker the walls of these containers, the longer they will generally last. Avoid placing metal containers (other than lead) in hot afternoon sun, where they'd heat up quickly and cook plant roots.

STONE

Many kinds of stone have been fashioned into garden containers over the years. Granite, marble, limestone, and alabaster pots and urns are expensive. Technology has made less expensive replicas available in synthetic stone. The imitations are often as lovely as the stone they simulate and are frequently much lighter in weight. Many plants appreciate the heat and lower humidity common in stone and stonelike containers. (Drainage, of course, is important; a drill and masonry bit or gravel and liner pots can remedy a deficiency of holes.)

WOOD

Wooden containers offer many advantages. Wood is a natural insulator, and it keeps roots relatively cool compared with those of plants growing in terra-cotta pots. Because soil temperatures inside wooden containers

Interesting wooden boxes have potential beyond the traditional window box.

fluctuate less from day to day, plants in them suffer less long-term stress. Wooden boxes allow less evaporation than terra cotta, so they're easier to keep watered. They are also durable. Less rigid and brittle than clay or concrete, they aren't as easily broken up by the expansion of freezing soil and may be left outside in winter with little damage. Some types of wood, such as redwood and cedar, are resistant to rot and will last without treatment for many years. When painted or otherwise waterproofed, other types of wood can also make durable planters. Wooden containers are a good choice for large plants. They're more affordable than enormous clay pots and easier to move, especially if equipped with casters.

PERMANENT PLANTERS

Large, immobile planters made of stone, brick, or heavy timber can be thought of as big, deep pots or small self-contained garden beds. Some are built with the house; others are added later, perhaps with a patio or deck. Permanent planters offer opportunities for mass plantings of one or two types of large plants, such as black-eyed Susans or big hostas. They can be treated as small beds composed of various combinations of annuals, perennials, shrubs, and trees.

Permanent planters, such as this one of brick, can be planted like large containers or small garden beds.

"FOUND" CONTAINERS

Gardeners have long made use of all sorts of castoffs as plant containers. Ingenuity can turn a rusting wheelbarrow, old crock, hollow tree stump, or vintage coal bucket into a perfect home for summer plants. Half whiskey barrels planted with everything from roses to peaches to lilies can make striking focal points; this American innovation is increasingly copied overseas. Bushel-basket planters, another uniquely American idea, are back in vogue.

Not all innovations have staying power. But much of the fun is in getting the nerve to try something new. Who knows what eye-catching container lurks in the shadows of your shed or basement, waiting to be filled with plants?

"Found" containers like this recycled bicycle can add surprise and humor to a garden.

designing the containers

CONTAINER DESIGN RANGES from the display of a single plant in a single pot to the orchestration of scores of plants in dozens of pots. For both extremes and in between, success requires forethought.

Many plants recommend themselves for the color, form, or fragrance of their flowers or foliage. An array of shapes adds variety, whether the plants are grown together in the same container or potted up separately and staged together. Round, mounded plants are enhanced by spiky, linear plants or by sprawlers and trailers. Airy, feathery plants need the contrast of dense, compact companions. Vase-shaped plants add grace, while fanciful shapes such as clipped topiary balls lend a degree of formality, if not a touch of whimsy. Tall plants and vines serve as screens or focal points. Whether you're displaying one plant or many, success depends as much on how they relate to their surroundings as on the qualities of the plants and pots themselves. Choose colors, shapes, and textures that complement your home and personality. Old-fashioned annuals and

Rhythmic repetition of colors and forms unifies a long container.

perennials suit a cottage-garden approach; striking, dramatic flowers and foliage enhance the lean look of modern architecture. Scale is as important as style. On its own outside a large formal entrance, a small pot of pansies will be lost; a small potted flowering tree, a tall clump of ornamental grass, or a staged grouping of a half-dozen pots would be more effective. Consider also the mood you wish to create. Reinforce the tranquility of a shady nook with an all white and green potted display; enliven a sunny patio or deck with a riotous blend of hot-colored flowers.

Where pots rest on the same level, plants of different heights as well as textures create an effective composition.

In general, a single plant should be about the same height as its pot.

INDIVIDUAL PLANTS

An eye-catching display of a single plant in a single pot (or a number of the same kind of plants in a single pot) has much to do with selecting the right pot for the plant. Perhaps one of the least effective displays is a tall pot planted with short annuals. As a general guideline for pleasing plant-to-pot proportions, single-specimen plants should be as tall as the pot they inhabit. (This is true of window boxes, urns, and other containers as well.) There are, of course, many exceptions to this principle. Succulents are often displayed in short, wide pots with their foliage forming low, thick clumps. Ornamental grasses and shrubs may be seven or eight times as tall as their containers. The idea is to select the container that best displays the distinctive form of the plant.

MIXING PLANTS IN ONE POT

A pot of mixed flowers and foliage is essentially a living bouquet. The number and variety of plants are limited by the size of the container, though you can generally put more plants in a pot designed for just a single season. Because annuals (and other plants grown as annuals) need only enough soil to see them through a few months, they can be spaced more closely than would otherwise be prudent. This is true also of annuals mixed with a single dominant perennial, shrub, or one flowering bulb. You will need to be generous with water and fertilizer to help alleviate conditions in their cramped quarters.

Create an eye-catching pot by combining plants with attributes that complement or contrast one another in a pleasing manner. Start by choosing a dominant plant as the centerpiece. Depending on the size of the

More is more: it's difficult to imagine fitting one more plant in this pot, and the effect is delightful.

container, this could be anything from a rosebush to a marguerite daisy to a fuchsia. Then design around this plant, just as you would plan a room around an important feature such as a sofa, rug, or china cabinet. Large permanent planters or long, narrow containers such as window boxes may have several focal points.

In a mixed container, consider plants that occupy different levels as well as orchestrating a color scheme, such as in this pleasing combination.

Simple combinations, such as this one of maiden grass (*Miscanthus sinensis* 'Bandwidth'), nemesia (*Nemesia strumosa* 'KLM'), and stonecrop (*Sedum rupestre* 'Angelina'), can be very attractive.

Pots of chrysanthemums march up a stairway.

GROUPS OF POTS

One beautifully designed container may stand on its own, or it may become part of a larger grouping clustered on stairs, a windowsill, or a patio. A line of identical pots and plants can edge a driveway or the railing of a deck, as well as leading the eye and visitors to your door or to an area of entertainment or recreation. Massed, multipot plantings of a single plant type can provide a bold accent near an entryway or by a garden seat.

Remember that in the confines of a small deck or balcony, a single large plant serves the same purpose a tree does in the yard—adding structure to the area, inviting an assortment of smaller companion plants. A few large specimens also add a more permanent feeling to a collection of potted plants. Large plants can serve as backdrops for smaller plants or as focal points, especially if they offer a flush of bloom, interesting leaves, or striking branching patterns.

For an informal look, select pots of varying sizes—some deeper than others, one or two perhaps that are quite a bit bigger than the rest. Mix square, rectangular, or other shapes with the round pots. Add a metal, stone, or wood container as an accent in a group of terra-cotta pots.

Large numbers of plants in a collection are often more attractive when grouped into sections rather than strung uniformly around the patio. Leave some area blank for visual relief. Imagine you are hanging a number of small pictures on your wall. The "one here and one there" approach looks busy, but group them together, with plenty of wall to "frame" them, and the whole collection is enhanced.

themes and seasons

GARDENERS WITH A PASSION for particular colors may use all styles of plant groupings—mixed pots, massing, and planters—to carry a theme throughout their property. For example, an aficionado of yellow flowers may feature that color everywhere, in sun or shade, and in every season, by positioning containers in strategic spots. Marigolds, lilies, and zinnias blaze in their sunny pots, while yellow tuberous begonias bloom in the shade. Primroses and daffodils grace the garden for winter or spring accents (depending on climate); golden mums glow in autumn.

Not only can you change the look of your garden with different plants and colors (almost like new slipcovers for indoor furniture), but you can echo the change of seasons. A springtime grouping of tulips and daffodils, for instance, gives way to bright petunias or bold cannas, concluding with chrysanthemums or ornamental kale. Designing container gardens is not solely a once-a-year activity. A creative gardener can paint an ever-changing picture throughout the year.

Whenever plants are grown in containers instead of an open garden, watering becomes very important, and in hot weather with warm air currents and a bright sun above, soil conditions demand that water is in good supply. But there is another problem that results from the continuing passage of water through the soil and what continuing watering does to the condition of that soil—fertilizers soon begin to be washed out of the soil and down through drain holes and that fertilizer needs to be replaced.

So, when summer suns shine above and watering of containers continues below on the porch, balcony, or deck, a good idea is to increase your use of a good liquid fertilizer, at least every three or four weeks. And instead of mixing the fertilizer straight from the package, instead of using the usual one tablespoon per gallon of water, use a half-tablespoon, but water with that solution at least once a month, and in areas of really hot weather, once every two or three weeks.

A lovely silver garden is much easier to accomplish in containers than in a garden bed.

FACING PAGE: Planned carefully, container plantings can change dramatically with the seasons. Here pansies give way to geraniums and golden oregano as spring moves to summer. In fall, the pots are changed to provide a tapestry of winter grasses and cuttings of magnolia, holly, and winterberry.

PLANTS

LEMON VERBENA

how to grow

Tolerates heat. Loam-based commercial soil mix. Best in a clay pot; 12-inch-by-12-inch pot at maturity. Damaged by standing water. Feed sparingly and cut off faded blooms. In cold climates, can overwinter in a bright, cool, dry place. May lose all its leaves, but continue to water sparingly, and look for new growth in spring.

A tender woody herb grown as an annual in cold climates. Bears open clusters of tiny lilac or white flowers in summer.

ALOYSIA CITRODORA

FULL SUN

ZONE 8

HEIGHT: 3–4 feet

SPREAD: to 2 feet

SNAPDRAGON

how to grow

Loam-based commercial soil mix. Sow seeds in shallow flats to germinate and grow at 60°F. Pinch seedlings to promote branching. In mild-winter areas, set out plants in early fall for winter or spring bloom. In colder regions, plant in early spring for spring or summer bloom. Cut back after blooming, and the plants will often bloom again.

Cheerful perennials or annuals with upright leafy stems and colorful two-lipped flowers; grows year-round in mild climates.

ANTIRRHINUM MAJUS

FULL OR PART SUN

ALL ZONES

HEIGHT: 6–36 inches

SPREAD: 8–18 inches

WAX BEGONIA

how to grow

Tolerates heat. Loam-based commercial soil mix. Can be crowded into mixed pots. Tolerates occasional dryness but can't take soggy conditions. Will burn badly in full sun if not watered regularly. Feed every 2 weeks.

A favorite for containers, these compact, leafy plants are covered with flowers for months on end. The fleshy stems branch repeatedly, making bushy mounds. The green, green and white, reddish purple, or bronze leaves always look fresh and shiny.

FLOWERING KALE, FLOWERING CABBAGE

how to grow

For good root penetration, use a loam-based commercial soil mix that is both free draining and on the light side. Sow seeds in summer, or buy plants to set out in early fall. Break up root balls when planting in final container. In hot weather spring-germinated plants are liable to bolt (a fancy way of saying they quickly go to seed); remove flower stalks to maintain form. Feed monthly using a slow-release fertilizer.

Looks like a giant crepe-paper flower, but the crinkly textured rosette is actually made of brightly colored leaves that stay crisp and colorful for months.

BRASSICA OLERACEA

FULL OR PART SUN
ALL ZONES
HEIGHT: 12 inches
SPREAD: 28 inches

BUSH VIOLET

how to grow

Loam-based commercial soil mix amended with organic matter to increase water retention, particularly in hanging baskets. Buy plants or start seeds indoors 8 to 10 weeks before last frost. Plant several to a 10-inch pot, or combine in a mixed container. Pinch to promote bushiness. Needs constant moisture—is easily damaged by drying out—but other than that, mostly trouble-free.

A small bushy plant with oval veined leaves, terrific trailer for hanging baskets. The showy, cool blue flowers bloom for a long time. 'Marine Bells' shown here.

BROWALLIA SPECIOSA

PART SUN TO SHADE

ZONE 10

HEIGHT: 12–24 inches

SPREAD: 12–18 inches

POT MARIGOLD

how to grow

Loam-based commercial soil mix. Tolerates some frost, so set out early. Easily stressed by drought. Does best in cool weather. Grow for summer bloom in the North, for fall to spring bloom where winters are mild. Deadhead to prolong blooming. Cut back and fertilize in midsummer to encourage fall bloom.

Bright and cheerful blossoms ranging from pale cream to yellow, gold, and bright orange make this an easy-to-grow annual.

CALENDULA OFFICINALIS

FULL OR PART SUN

ALL ZONES

HEIGHT: to 2 feet

SPREAD: 8–12 inches

ORNAMENTAL PEPPER

how to grow

Tolerates heat. Loam-based commercial soil mix. Put one plant per 6-inch pot or add to mixed container. Start seeds indoors 6 to 8 weeks before last frost; set outside after night temperatures rise above 55°F. Needs constant moisture. Bring inside when frost threatens for a few more weeks of show. While not poisonous, these peppers usually lack flavor or are too hot for most tastes.

Ornamental peppers, with their dark green oval leaves, small white flowers, and showy fruits, can strike a note of surprise in mixed containers.

CAPSICUM ANNUUM

FULL SUN

ALL ZONES

HEIGHT: 8–14 inches

SPREAD: 8–12 inches

MADAGASCAR PERIWINKLE

how to grow

Loam-based commercial soil mix. Transplant seedlings carefully (they can be shocked by rough handling), about 5 inches apart after danger of frost is past. Needs regular watering but rots if overwatered.

Grows quickly from seed to make a mounding bushy plant of glossy green foliage covered with cheerful five-petaled flowers in shades of white, pink, or rose, often with a contrasting eye.

CATHARANTHUS ROSEUS

FULL OR PART SUN

ALL ZONES

HEIGHT: 1–2 feet

SPREAD: 1 foot or more

FEVERFEW

how to grow

Seedlings grow quickly; use a 10-inch-by-10-inch pot for small nursery-grown plants. Cut back after flowering to encourage repeat bloom. Can overwinter in cold frame or cool greenhouse.

Carefree and easy to grow, with pungently aromatic ferny foliage and masses of ½-inch daisies off and on all summer and fall.

CHRYSANTHEMUM PARTHENIUM

FULL OR PART SUN

ZONE 5

HEIGHT: 1–3 feet

SPREAD: 1–2 feet

DAHLIAS

how to grow

American native plants that approve of heat. Add organic material such as manure, compost, or leaf mold for moisture retention, and coarse sand to improve drainage. Plant tubers about 6 inches below the rim of a deep pot, cover with 1 inch of soil, then add soil as shoots grow. Plants need constant moisture; they do not tolerate drought. Fertilize heavily for best flower production. Pinch tips for bushy plants with many smaller blossoms; remove side shoots and buds to produce fewer, larger blossoms. Dig tubers in fall, dry and brush off soil, store in a cool but frost-free and dark place surrounded by organic material such as wood shavings. Sprinkle occasionally with water to avoid desiccation; if rot appears, dispose of the infected tubers. In spring, carefully separate the tubers and replant those with the most vigorous buds and shoots.

Remarkable for their bright blossoms that come in many colors, dahlias add pizzazz to a container garden from midsummer on, when other plants may be past their prime.

FULL SUN
ALL ZONES
HEIGHT: 1–6 feet
SPREAD: 1–3 feet

FUCHSIA

how to grow

Soilless or loam-based commercial soil mix amended with plenty of organic matter and coarse sand for rapid drainage. Won't tolerate hot sun or dry air. You can grow them as annuals in pots as small as 4 to 6 inches. Large plants grown as perennials, including standards, require a 12- to 14-inch pot. Keep moist. Early in season, pinch tips often to promote branching. Cut perennials back to main framework branches in early spring. Fertilize lightly every 2 weeks.

Most are tender evergreen shrubs or small trees with simple leaves and showy flowers that dangle like earrings from the stems.

FUCHSIA HYBRIDS

PART SUN TO SHADE

ALL ZONES

HEIGHT: varies

SPREAD: varies

GERBERA DAISY

how to grow

Soilless or loam-based commercial soil mix. Pots 6 to 8 inches wide accommodate largest plants. When planting, do not cover the crown, and don't let soil wash in and cover crown later. Water regularly and fertilize frequently. If growing it as a perennial, divide older plants in early spring, keeping several crowns per division. Seeds are expensive, but seedlings may bloom the first year. Overwinter indoors as a houseplant, giving it bright light and cool (60°F) nights.

The most aristocratic and shapely daisy, a good container plant, and an excellent cut flower with nice long stalks.

GERBERA JAMESONII

FULL OR PART SHADE

ZONE 9

HEIGHT: to 18 inches

SPREAD: to 18 inches

HELIOTROPE

how to grow

Loam-based commercial soil mix amended with organic material such as manure, compost, or leaf mold. If grown as a perennial, plants can reach 3 feet or more, so eventually they might need a 1-gallon pot. Provide constant moisture (performs well in high humidity). Easy from seed and cuttings (summer or fall). Overwinter on sun porch, in greenhouse, under lights, or in bright window; ease back on water and fertilizer; will drop leaves.

This rather bushy shrub produces tight flat clusters of tiny lavender or purple flowers prized for their sweet "cherry pie" scent. 'Marine Lemoine Strain' shown here.

HELIOTROPIUM ARBORESCENS

FULL SUN

ZONE 10

HEIGHT: 12–36 inches

SPREAD: 10–24 inches

TRAILING LANTANA

how to grow

Tolerates heat. Loam-based commercial soil mix. Grown as an annual, it will thrive in a 6- to 8-inch pot; as a standard or shrub, use a 12- to 16-inch pot. Feed lightly. Pinch frequently to keep plant bushy. Tolerates salt along the coasts. Overwinter indoors or in greenhouse. If left outside in milder climates, it may freeze back in cold winters but will recover from base. Prune hard in spring to remove damaged wood; shape as desired.

One of the few good hanging-basket plants for hot, dry, windy locations, trailing lantana has sprawling stems and lavender blossoms that bloom throughout the growing season. (A white variety is also available.)

LANTANA MONTEVIDENSIS

FULL SUN

ZONE 7

HEIGHT: 6–18 inches

SPREAD: to 3 feet

EDGING LOBELIA

how to grow

Soilless commercial mix provides the light, freely draining medium plants prefer. Clay pots aerate roots best. Doesn't like hot summers but can succeed if it is established before hot weather begins, shaded from afternoon sun, and regularly watered. Start seeds indoors 10 to 12 weeks before last frost. Sow on soil surface; seeds are tiny and need light to germinate. Set plants in display containers after danger of frost is past. Space 6 to 9 inches apart; don't crowd (trailers especially). Never allow to dry out, but excessive watering causes molds and rotting. Feed monthly. Shear back partway in midsummer to rejuvenate plants if flowering slows.

Blooms throughout summer and fall, with tiny irregular flowers in all shades from light to dark blue, and also white and wine red. 'Sapphire Blue' shown here.

LOBELIA ERINUS

FULL SUN OR PART SHADE

ALL ZONES

HEIGHT: 4–8 inches

SPREAD: to 12 inches

SWEET ALYSSUM

how to grow

Tolerates heat. Loam-based commercial soil mix. Start seeds indoors 6 weeks before last frost or sow direct. Shear back halfway when plants get tatty in midsummer, and they will be renewed.

Indispensable for containers, this adaptable annual forms a spreading mound or mat of branching stems with tiny leaves and masses of four-petaled flowers in shades of white, pink, rose, or purple. 'Snow Princess' shown here.

LOBULARIA MARITIMA

FULL SUN

ALL ZONES

HEIGHT: to 6 inches

SPREAD: 12 inches

FLOWERING TOBACCO

how to grow

Tolerates heat. Loam-based commercial soil mix. Seeds are small, like those of petunias. Sow indoors at 70°F 6 to 8 weeks before last frost. Pinch when potting plants to encourage bushy growth. Feed in midsummer when heat is highest. Cut off spent flower stalks to reduce seeding and to renew bloom.

Blooms reliably all summer long in shades of white, pink, rose, lavender, red, crimson, or chartreuse. Flowers are like 1-inch stars with long tubular throats, borne on erect branching stalks.

NICOTIANA ALATA

FULL OR PART SUN

ALL ZONES

HEIGHT: 1–3 feet

SPREAD: 1 foot

SWEET BASIL

how to grow

Tolerates heat. Loam-based commercial soil mix. Use one plant per 8- to 10-inch pot; can crowd with other annuals in larger pots. Keep moist. Prefers hot weather. Easy from seed, started indoors 8 weeks before last frost, or sown direct. Pinch for bushiness.

As indispensable as tomatoes for summer cuisine, basil is a bushy herb with shiny, wonderfully fragrant leaves.

OCIMUM BASILICUM

FULL OR PART SUN

ALL ZONES

HEIGHT: to 2 feet

SPREAD: 1 foot

COMMON GERANIUM

how to grow

Tolerates heat. Soilless or loam-based commercial soil mix that drains well. Use a 4- to 12-inch pot. Feed weekly with a dilute fertilizer solution. Plants are compact when you buy them but may get straggly later unless you keep pruning and pinching the tips. Root tip cuttings in late summer to overwinter indoors on a sunny windowsill, or stop watering, and cut stems back to roots and stubs, storing them by hanging in bunches in a cool cellar or frost-free garage. In Zone 9, geraniums are hardy outdoors.

One of the best and easiest flowering plants for pots, window boxes, and planters. Makes big spherical clusters of 1-inch-wide flowers in many shades of red, pink, salmon, or white.

PELARGONIUM X HORTORUM

FULL SUN

ALL ZONES

HEIGHT: 6–48 inches

SPREAD: 6–48 inches

SCENTED GERANIUMS

how to grow

Tolerates heat. Soilless or loam-based commercial soil mix that drains well. Use a 4- to 12-inch pot. Feed biweekly with a dilute fertilizer solution. Can stand crowded pots if well fed and watered. Overwinter well on windowsill or in sunroom.

The dozens of species and hybrids, grown for their attractive and strongly scented foliage, have delicate white, pink, or lavender flowers too. They bloom in winter or spring.

PELARGONIUM SPP.

FULL SUN

ALL ZONES

HEIGHT: varies

SPREAD: 1½–2 feet

COMMON GARDEN PETUNIA

how to grow

Tolerates hot and cool weather. Loam-based commercial soil mix. Start tiny seeds indoors 8 weeks before last frost. Use one to three plants in a 12-inch hanging basket. Fertilize monthly. Frequent deadheading prolongs bloom, and frequent pinching makes plants bushier. Shear back in midsummer and fertilize heavily if flower production has slowed.

Blooming profusely for months, the round flowers are single or double, in shades of red, rose, pink, purple, violet-blue, pale yellow, white, or striped combinations.

PETUNIA X HYBRIDA

FULL OR PART SUN

ALL ZONES

HEIGHT: 1–3 feet

SPREAD: 1–3 feet

COLEUS

how to grow

Tolerates heat. Loam-based commercial soil mix. Start seeds indoors 8 weeks before last frost, or buy plants at local nurseries. Set outside when night temperatures stay above 50°F. To encourage compact, bushy plants, pinch tips and remove flower buds as they form. Can be crowded into a pot. Keep soil moist and feed often with high-nitrogen liquid fertilizer. Overwinter on a sunny windowsill or take cuttings and root them in a glass of water to save favorite plants from year to year.

There are hundreds of cultivars and seed strains. Some are more compact; some are multicolored; some have fringed or ruffled leaves. Leaf colors include green, chartreuse, yellow, cream, pink, salmon, orange, and red.

PLECTRANTHUS SCUTELLARIOIDES

PART SUN OR FILTERED SHADE

ALL ZONES

HEIGHT: 1–2 feet

SPREAD: 1–2 feet

MOSS ROSE

how to grow

Tolerates heat. Loam-based commercial soil mix. Flat pots are fine for this shallow-rooting plant; space 3 to 4 inches apart for immediate effect. Buy plants in spring or direct-sow seeds about the time of last frost. Seeds are tiny, but seedlings grow fast. Water regularly until plants are established. Shear halfway back and fertilize in midsummer to promote fresh growth and to renew flowering.

The trailing stems are covered with plump cylindrical leaves and waxy round flowers, 1 inch wide, single or double, in shades of yellow, orange, red, pink, or white. 'Mojave Tangerine' shown here.

PORTULACA GRANDIFLORA

FULL SUN

ALL ZONES

HEIGHT: under 1 foot

SPREAD: 1 foot

MEALY BLUE SAGE

how to grow

Tolerates heat. Loam-based commercial soil mix. Start seeds indoors 8 weeks before last frost. Gets lush with regular watering. Pinch for bushy growth. Keeps blooming even if you don't remove old flower stalks. Overwinter indoors in sunny spot; cut back hard in spring.

Blooms and blooms from late spring to hard frost. Branches near the base and makes many upright stalks with small gray-green leaves on the bottom and crowded spikes of violet-blue flowers on top. 'Sallyfun Blue' shown here.

FRENCH MARIGOLD

how to grow

Tolerates heat. Soilless commercial mix. Direct-sow seeds, or start indoors 4 to 6 weeks before last frost. Use one plant per 8-inch pot or three in a 12-inch pot. Pinch off tips and first few flowers to promote bushiness. Leggy or top-heavy plants are liable to tip over in summer storms. Deadheading helps improve appearance and prolong bloom.

The single or double flower heads, 1 to 3 inches wide, come in shades of yellow, orange, red, mahogany, or bicolor. Flowers from early summer until frost whether you deadhead it or not.

TAGETES PATULA

FULL SUN

ALL ZONES

HEIGHT: 6–14 inches

SPREAD: 8–14 inches

NASTURTIUM

how to grow

Loam-based commercial soil mix; blooms best in poor soil. Seeds are large enough that children can handle them easily. Nasturtiums do not transplant well. Direct-sow in display pot or hanging basket in early spring, covering ½ inch deep, or start in peat pots. Thin to 6 to 12 inches apart. Keep moist. Fertilize sparingly—too much makes leaves at the expense of flowers.

Large, long-stalked flowers have a spicy fragrance and come in bright shades of yellow, orange, red, mahogany, cream, or bicolor. 'Alaska' shown here.

TROPAEOLUM MAJUS

FULL OR PART SUN

ALL ZONES

HEIGHT: 1 foot

SPREAD: 2 feet or more

GARDEN VERBENA

how to grow

Tolerates heat. Loam-based commercial soil mix amended with coarse sand to improve drainage. Seeds are difficult to germinate; it's easier to buy transplants, and garden centers have mixed or solid-color packs. Plants can be crowded in mixed pots. Deadhead to prolong bloom. Some gardeners take cuttings of favorites to winter over.

The starry flowers form dense round clusters, 2 to 3 inches wide, in bright shades of red, pink, purple, or white.

VERBENA X HYBRIDA

FULL SUN OR AFTERNOON SHADE

ALL ZONES

HEIGHT: 6–12 inches

SPREAD: 12 inches

PANSY

how to grow

Loam-based commercial soil mix. Start seeds or purchase plants for spring or fall display. Fall-planted seedlings overwinter with no protection even in Zone 6 and start blooming earlier than spring transplants. Don't let them dry out; feed regularly. Pinch back and feed when they get straggly. Deadhead or they'll stop blooming.

The wide (1- to 4-inch), flat, facelike flowers are loaded with personality and come in a very wide range of colors—red, pink, yellow, white, blue, and mahogany, usually marked with dark blotches.

VIOLA X WITTROCKIANA

FULL SUN OR AFTERNOON SHADE

ALL ZONES

HEIGHT: to 12 inches

SPREAD: to 12 inches

COMMON ZINNIA

how to grow

Tolerates heat. Loam-based commercial soil mix. Can be crowded in a mixed pot. Start seeds indoors 6 weeks before last frost. Doesn't grow well until the weather is warm. Requires no deadheading. Recovers from drying out. They don't tolerate dryness—watch those planted in clay containers closely. Don't crowd together with plants of similar height, so that air can circulate freely around the foliage.

There are dozens of strains to choose from. Most have double flowers, ranging from 1 to 6 inches wide, available in many colors.

BEAR'S BREECH

how to grow

Tolerates heat but not desert heat in sun. Loam-based commercial soil mix; 8- to 12-inch pot. Ordinary watering. Fertilize only to maintain good color. Easy to propagate by dividing rhizome. Goes dormant after blooming; in mild areas, remove flower spike and water during the summer to maintain leaves. In cold climates, overwinter in basement.

Dozens of whitish, lilac, or rose flowers with green or purplish bracts crowd robust spikes, up to 6 feet tall, from late spring to early summer.

ACANTHUS MOLLIS

SUN TO SHADE

ZONE 6

HEIGHT: 1½–2 feet

SPREAD: 3–4 feet

YARROW

how to grow

Soilless commercial mix in a clay pot; use a 12-inch pot for a single specimen. Tolerates dry heat but gets foliar diseases in hot, humid, rainy areas. Doesn't tolerate overwatering. Divide in spring every 2 to 3 years. Overwinter dormant plant in clay pot in cold but frost-free spot. Keep soil on the dry side.

A basal mound of soft, finely dissected gray leaves combines with pure lemon yellow flowers, borne in 2-inch clusters on 2-foot stalks to harmonize with most other perennials.

ACHILLEA 'MOONSHINE'

FULL SUN

ZONE 3

HEIGHT: 2 feet

SPREAD: 18 inches

BUGLEWEED, CARPET BUGLE

how to grow

Loam-based commercial soil mix. Ordinary watering; slow-release fertilizers work well. Use an 8-inch pot for a single specimen; three plants to a 12-inch pot. As companion plants, space small-leaved cultivars 6 inches apart; give larger ones 8 inches or more. *A. reptans* is invasive; prune runners to keep in bounds.

The smooth, shiny, wavy-margined leaves are green, purple, bronze, or variegated in gray, white, cream, or pink and provide color interest for a long season. 'Bronze Beauty' shown here.

AJUGA REPTANS

SUN TO SHADE

ZONE 3

HEIGHT: 4–8 inches

SPREAD: 8 inches or more

CHIVES

how to grow

Tolerates heat. Loam-based commercial soil mix. Easy from seed started indoors or out in spring. Divide an old clump in early spring into dozens of new starts. Shear after flowering to tidy up plant and to promote new growth. Overwinter on windowsill or in cold frame. Long-lived and trouble-free.

The lavender flowers in 1-inch-wide heads on stiff stalks last a month in late spring; they also make good cut flowers, can be dried for winter bouquets, and look pretty (but taste chaffy) in salads.

ALLIUM SCHOENOPRASUM

FULL OR PART SUN

ZONE 3

HEIGHT: 12 inches

SPREAD: 18 inches

ARTEMESIA

how to grow

Tolerates heat. Loam-based commercial soil mix. Start with a 1-gallon pot from the nursery and move up gradually, repotting in spring. Trim back old shoots to force new growth in spring. In cold climates, overwinter indoors or in a cold frame. Easily propagated by cuttings taken in midsummer.

Forms a generous mound of silvery filigree foliage that is striking at dusk or under patio lights.

ARTEMESIA 'POWIS CASTLE'

SUN TO SHADE

ZONE 6

HEIGHT: 2–3 feet

SPREAD: 2–4 feet

ASTILBE

how to grow

Best with a soil mix of garden loam and organic material such as manure, compost, or leaf mold. Mature plants need at least a gallon-sized pot at maturity. Plants need constant moisture. Fertilize with formula for acid-loving plants. Protect from hot afternoon sun. (Astilbes do best in cool summers and are poor choices for hot, semiarid areas.) Divide crowded clumps in spring. In winter, store the dormant clumps in their pots in a cold frame or trench in the garden.

The foliage is deep green to bronze, and the flowers come in shades of white, pale to dark pink, and deep purplish and carmine reds, opening between June and September; spent flowers turn reddish brown and remain attractive for months.

ASTILBE X ARENDSII HYBRIDS

PART SUN TO SHADE

ZONE 2

HEIGHT: 2–3 feet

SPREAD: 2–3 feet

JAPANESE PAINTED FERN

how to grow

Soilless commercial mix amended with humus. Use one plant per 8- to 10-inch pot. Place crown on top of soil and cover with mulch. Needs constant moisture. Old fronds make an excellent mulch, or you can remove them after all danger of frost is past. You can divide mature plants in early spring or late fall. Protect roots from freezing in winter.

This is one of America's most popular garden ferns, its triangular fronds tricolored in burgundy, silver-gray, and green. These ferns will occasionally produce baby ferns.

ATHYRIUM GOERINGIANUM 'PICTUM'

SHADE

ZONE 5

HEIGHT: 12–18 inches

SPREAD: 18 inches

HEARTLEAF BERGENIA

how to grow

Loam-based commercial soil mix. Large pot (12 inches) will minimize winter freeze-thaw damage. Divide crowded plantings in spring or fall. In Zone 5 and north, overwinter in cool greenhouse or cold frame.

This hardy and vigorous perennial forms a clump of large, thick, cabbagelike leaves, waxy and green in summer, turning rich glossy red in fall as the temperature starts to drop. Nodding clusters of pink flowers rise barely above the leaves in spring.

BERGENIA CORDIFOLIA

PART SHADE

ZONE 3

HEIGHT: 12–18 inches

SPREAD: 12–24 inches

SERBIAN BELLFLOWER

how to grow

Loam-based commercial soil mix; must be well drained. Fertilize regularly, deadhead, and trim stems as needed. Easy to grow from cuttings or divisions. Overwinter in cold frame or cool greenhouse.

Long trailing stems spread rapidly from a central mound to dangle from a hanging basket or other container. Plants are covered with loose clusters of starry lavender-blue or white flowers in spring. 'Blue Waterfall' shown here.

CAMPANULA POSCHARSKYANA

FULL OR PART SUN

ZONE 3

HEIGHT: 6–9 inches

SPREAD: 12 inches or more

DWARF PLUMBAGO

how to grow

Tolerates heat if partly shaded. Loam-based commercial soil mix. Put one plant per 10-inch pot; three plants in a 14-inch pot. Cut old stems to the ground in spring. Rooted runners can be transplanted in spring or fall. Space 8 inches apart for a ground cover. Divide in spring; discard woody old crowns, save vigorous young shoots. Goes dormant in winter even in the mildest climates. Overwinter in unheated garage; keep soil on the dry side.

A spreading perennial with clear blue flowers, ½ inch wide and borne in dense heads. Leaves are smooth and plain, dark green in summer and reddish purple in fall.

CERATOSTIGMA PLUMBAGINOIDES

FULL OR PART SUN

ZONE 5

HEIGHT: 12 inches

SPREAD: 12 inches or more

FLORIST'S CHRYSANTHEMUM

how to grow

Soilless or loam-based commercial soil mix; should drain well. Pot individual plants in 4- to 6-inch pots, depending on your needs. Space 6 to 8 inches apart in window boxes or big pots. Keep moist—water stress causes plants to lose lower leaves. Frequent light feeding. Pinch tips back hard two or three times to shape low growers into dense bushy mounds. Stake tall forms if you want straight stems, and remove side buds if you want just one big flower per stalk. After flowering, cut stalks back to 6-inch stubs and store in an unheated garage or a cold frame over winter. In spring, divide clump into separate rooted shoots or root tip cuttings. Several strains of hardy chrysanthemums can be raised easily from seed and will blossom the first year from an early-spring sowing.

There's an endless array of cultivars, colored white, yellow, bronze, orange, pink, red, or purple, sometimes with two or more colors in the same flower.

CHRYSANTHEMUM X MORIFOLIUM

FULL SUN OR LIGHT SHADE

HARDINESS DEPENDS ON CULTIVAR

HEIGHT: 6 inches–6 feet

SPREAD: 1–5 feet or more

THREAD-LEAVED COREOPSIS

how to grow

Tolerates heat. Soilless or loam-based commercial soil mix; needs good drainage and will recover from drying out. Divide and repot every 3 years to maintain vigor. There are too many flowers to deadhead individually, but you can trim off the top of the plant to encourage a second bloom. Poor drainage and waterlogging lead to mildew and other problems.

Valued for its deeply divided, fine, feathery foliage and pale golden yellow blossoms, 1 to 2 inches wide, borne for 4 to 6 weeks in midsummer.

COREOPSIS VERTICILLATA

FULL SUN

ZONE 3

HEIGHT: 2–3 feet

SPREAD: 2–3 feet

PURPLE ICE PLANT

how to grow

Tolerates heat. Loam-based commercial soil mix with coarse sand added for good drainage. Flattish bowls and pans of terra cotta are good containers. Can survive drying out and general negligence once established. Cuttings root easily. In cold climates, overwinter in cold frame or cool greenhouse.

Brilliant flowers are dazzling on a sunny patio. Narrow succulent leaves are sprinkled with bright magenta daisylike flowers from June until frost.

DELOSPEMIA COOPERI

FULL SUN

ZONE 6 OR 5

HEIGHT: 2–4 inches

SPREAD: 12 inches

HARDY AGERATUM

how to grow

Tolerates heat. Loam-based commercial soil mix. Use one plant per 12-inch pot. Feed with slow-release fertilizer. Remove spent flowers to limit self-seeding. Divide every 2 to 3 years in spring when new shoots emerge. Overwinter dormant plant in unheated garage or cold frame.

Branched clusters of fluffy powder blue flowers enliven the garden for 4 to 6 weeks in late summer and fall.

EUPATORIUM COELESTINUM

FULL OR PART SUN

ZONE 6

HEIGHT: 18–24 inches

SPREAD: 2 feet or more

BLUE FESCUE

how to grow

Soilless commercial mix. Put one plant in an 8-inch pot, or space 8 to 10 inches apart in a planter. Allow soil to become slightly dry between waterings. Cut back once a year, in fall or spring. Clumps can (and should) go years without division. Overwinter in cold frame; keep soil dry.

A small clumping grass; while blue flowers come and go, this plant's blue foliage remains through the growing season and into winter.

FESTUCA OVINA VAR. GLAUCA

FULL SUN

ZONE 4

HEIGHT: 6–12 inches

SPREAD: 8–10 inches

FIREBUSH, HUMMINGBIRD BUSH

how to grow

Tolerates heat. Loam-based commercial soil mix. Shouldn't get too dry; feed regularly through summer. Shear to control shape and height and to promote perpetual bloom. Cut back to the ground after fall frost. Overwinter in greenhouse or on sun porch in the North.

The red to red-orange flowers are tubular, about 2 inches long, dropping quickly but constantly replaced by new buds. The dark green leaves turn red-orange in fall.

HAMELIA PATENS

FULL OR PART SUN

ZONE 8

HEIGHT: 2–3 feet

SPREAD: 2–3 feet

LENTEN ROSE

how to grow

Loam-based commercial soil mix amended with plenty of organic matter and coarse sand to improve drainage. Ordinary watering okay. One plant per pot. *H. orientalis* is easy to grow from seed—in late summer you often find baby plants growing underneath mother plants. Other species can be more difficult, but worth the effort. If moved or divided, hellebores reestablish slowly, so be patient. Remove old leaves in spring before flowering; shiny new ones will soon take their place.

Clusters of several nodding, cup-shaped flowers, 2 to 3 inches wide, open in early spring. Flowers come in many shades of pink, plum, white, or chartreuse speckled with maroon.

HELLEBORUS ORIENTALIS

PART SUN TO SHADE

ZONE 5

HEIGHT: 18–24 inches

SPREAD: 24 inches

HYBRID DAYLILIES

how to grow

Soilless or loam-based commercial soil mix amended with organic matter and coarse sand to improve drainage. Don't bury plant's crown, which can rot with constant watering in the container. Don't let soil dry out completely. Remove spent flowers and flower stems. Some daylilies multiply fast enough to be divided every few years; others can grow undisturbed for decades. Divide crowded plants in spring or fall and repot. In areas with very low winter temperatures, store in frost-free location.

Each flower lasts only a day, but new buds open over a period of weeks. Flowers range from 2 to 7 inches wide, in shades of cream, yellow, orange, salmon, pink, rose, brick red, purplish red, lavender, or green. There are thousands of daylily varieties and plants grow easily from seed.

HEMEROCALLIS HYBRIDS

FULL SUN

ZONE 4

HEIGHT: 1–6 feet

SPREAD: 15 inches–2 feet or more

CORALBELLS, ALUMROOT

how to grow

Loam-based commercial soil mix amended with organic matter to increase water retention; neutral to slightly alkaline pH is ideal. Clay or wooden containers help by allowing freer movement of air. Position crown level with soil surface. When watering, try to keep crown from remaining too moist. Remove entire stalks of faded flowers to prolong bloom. If you overwinter outside, mulch to prevent frost heaving—plants tend to shove up out of the soil and must be reset. Keep soil on the dry side over winter. Divide every few years in early spring.

Makes a compact mound of thick, leathery, almost evergreen leaves, which may be round or kidney-shaped, toothed or lobed, crimped or ruffled. The wiry leafless stalks hold tiny pink, red, or creamy white flowers well above the foliage, forming an airy cloud of bloom.

HEUCHERA HYBRIDS

FULL SUN OR PART SHADE

ZONE 4

HEIGHT: 12 inches (foliage) to 18 inches (flowers)

SPREAD: 12–18 inches

HOSTAS

how to grow

Soilless or loam-based commercial soil mix amended with organic matter and coarse sand to improve drainage. Pot size varies (from 4 to 12 inches or so) with plant size. Hostas are most luxuriant if soil is constantly moist; a generous layer of mulch helps retain soil moisture.

Hostas rarely need division; they can live for years in one pot. If you want to multiply your stock, knock a big plant out of its pot in spring when leaves first emerge. Cut or pull clump into smaller clusters, each with several shoots and plenty of roots. If necessary, hostas can be transplanted or divided later in the growing season. Just be sure to keep them well watered afterward. Overwinter outside or in garage or cold frame.

Perennials that make neat clumps of broad-bladed leaves. The small lilylike flowers are usually violet, blue, or white, sometimes very fragrant.

HOSTA SPECIES AND CULTIVARS

PART OR FULL SHADE

ZONE 4

HEIGHT: 6 inches–3 feet (foliage)

SPREAD: most are wider than they are tall

ENGLISH LAVENDER

how to grow

Loam-based commercial soil mix amended with coarse sand to increase drainage. Prefers a clay pot and crowded conditions; no larger than a 6-inch pot for a single plant. Pinch early to encourage full, dense habit. Allow to dry out between waterings. Feed frugally. In containers, it is best treated as an annual and grown from seed each year.

Prized for the legendary fragrance of its small lavender-purple flowers, which form crowded spikes on slender stalks in early summer.

LAVANDULA ANGUSTIFOLIA

FULL SUN

ZONE 5

HEIGHT: 1½ feet

SPREAD: 1 foot

LILYTURF

how to grow

Tolerates full shade, but most cultivars don't bloom as well, and variegated forms may turn green in shade. Loam-based commercial soil mix amended with coarse sand for improved drainage. Firm soil around transplants. Needs constant water to become established; tolerates short dry spells after first summer. After several years, divide crowded clumps anytime during growing season. Cut shabby old foliage in late winter prior to appearance of new growth.

Makes numerous slender spikes, 12 to 18 inches tall, of small lavender or white flowers in summer, followed by shiny, round blue-black berries.

LIRIOPE MUSCARI

PART SUN

ZONE 5

HEIGHT: 1–2 feet

SPREAD: to 1 foot

LEMON BALM

how to grow

Loam-based commercial soil mix. Best in a small container (6 inch maximum); tends to look weedy if given too much room. Don't overwater (no drip irrigation). Propagate by dividing clumps in spring. Pinch when young to encourage branching, then shear two or three times during the season to renew foliage; don't shear if you like the white flowers. Will stay green over winter and can be left outdoors to resprout in spring.

Very easy to grow, with a wonderful lemony aroma and flavor. Invasive in the ground or when grown with others in a window box or planter, it minds its manners on its own in a pot and makes a bushy mound if pruned repeatedly.

MELISSA OFFICINALIS

PART SUN

ZONE 5

HEIGHT: 2 feet

SPREAD: to 2 feet

PINEAPPLE MINT

how to grow

Loam-based commercial soil mix. One plant per large pot. Prune hard every few months to rejuvenate. Recovers from drying out. Feed twice a month. Overwinters outdoors, in a cellar, or on a windowsill.

The white-variegated form of pineapple mint is the most ornamental of all mints and has bright green and white leaves about 1 inch long. The flavor is mild, but the leaves make a pretty, edible garnish for beverages or salads.

MENTHA SUAVEOLENS

SUN TO SHADE

ZONE 5

HEIGHT: 1 foot or more

SPREAD: to 3 feet

SWORD FERN

how to grow

Soilless commercial mix. Mature plant needs an 8-inch or larger pot. Requires constant moisture, but don't overwater. Divide when crowded. Doesn't tolerate frost; overwinter indoors as a houseplant.

A common and easy-to-grow container fern. Bright green fronds arch and droop nicely over the edge of a hanging pot or fern stand.

NEPHROLEPIS EXALTATA

SHADE

ZONE 9

HEIGHT: to 5 feet

SPREAD: forms patch

GARDEN SAGE

how to grow

Loam-based commercial soil mix amended with coarse sand for good drainage. An 8- to 10-inch pot should accommodate the largest plants. Recovers from drying out. Feed lightly through growing season, especially if you're harvesting leaves. Cut back frozen shoots in late spring, before new growth starts, and remove faded blooms in summer. Divide every few years; plants aren't long-lived. Take root cuttings to overwinter tender cultivars, or buy new plants in spring.

The fragrant gray-green leaves of this favorite herb are used for seasoning and to make a therapeutic tea. Tall spikes of blue-purple flowers are colorful for weeks in early summer.

SALVIA OFFICINALIS

FULL SUN

ZONE 5

HEIGHT: 2 feet

SPREAD: 2 feet

STONECROP

how to grow

An adaptable plant; prefers full sun and well-drained, gritty potting soil (soilless commercial mix will do) but does well even in somewhat moist soil and part shade. Plant one per pot or at least 2 feet apart in large planters. Leave dry stems and seed heads to look at into winter, then cut back and store in cold frame or unheated garage. Divide clumps every third year to keep them from flopping open when they flower.

Forms a spreading clump of thick stems surrounded with plump, succulent leaves. The tiny starry flowers form clusters like broccoli, 4 to 6 inches wide, starting out pink, then deepening to dark salmon and finally rusty red.

SEDUM 'AUTUMN JOY'

FULL OR PART SUN
ZONE 3
HEIGHT: 1½–2 feet
SPREAD: 1½–2 feet

HEN-AND-CHICKS

how to grow

Loam-based commercial soil mix. Space 6 inches apart and they'll fill in by midsummer. Recovers from drying out; doesn't need to be fed regularly. Very easy and trouble-free. In harsh climates you may need to store in shady, protected area—snow cover is useful—or in cold frame.

Each "hen" rosette spreads 4 to 6 inches wide and is closely surrounded by many smaller "chicks." Flat clusters of starry reddish flowers top thick stems that stick up like chimneys.

SEMPERVIVUM TECTORUM

FULL OR PART SUN

ZONE 4

HEIGHT: 4 inches (foliage)

SPREAD: 1 foot or more

LEMON THYME

how to grow

Soilless commercial mix amended with coarse sand to improve drainage. One plant per 8-inch clay pot. Established plants can tolerate considerable dryness but can't take soggy soil, especially in winter. Shear after flowering to reduce self-seeding and to promote new growth. Feed with slow-release fertilizer in spring; add liquid supplement if you harvest leaves. Overwinter in cold frame or unheated garage; water sparingly. Cut back in early spring, removing damaged and old woody stems.

Makes a low, spreading mound of tiny glossy dark green leaves with a distinct lemony fragrance. Flowers are pale purple.

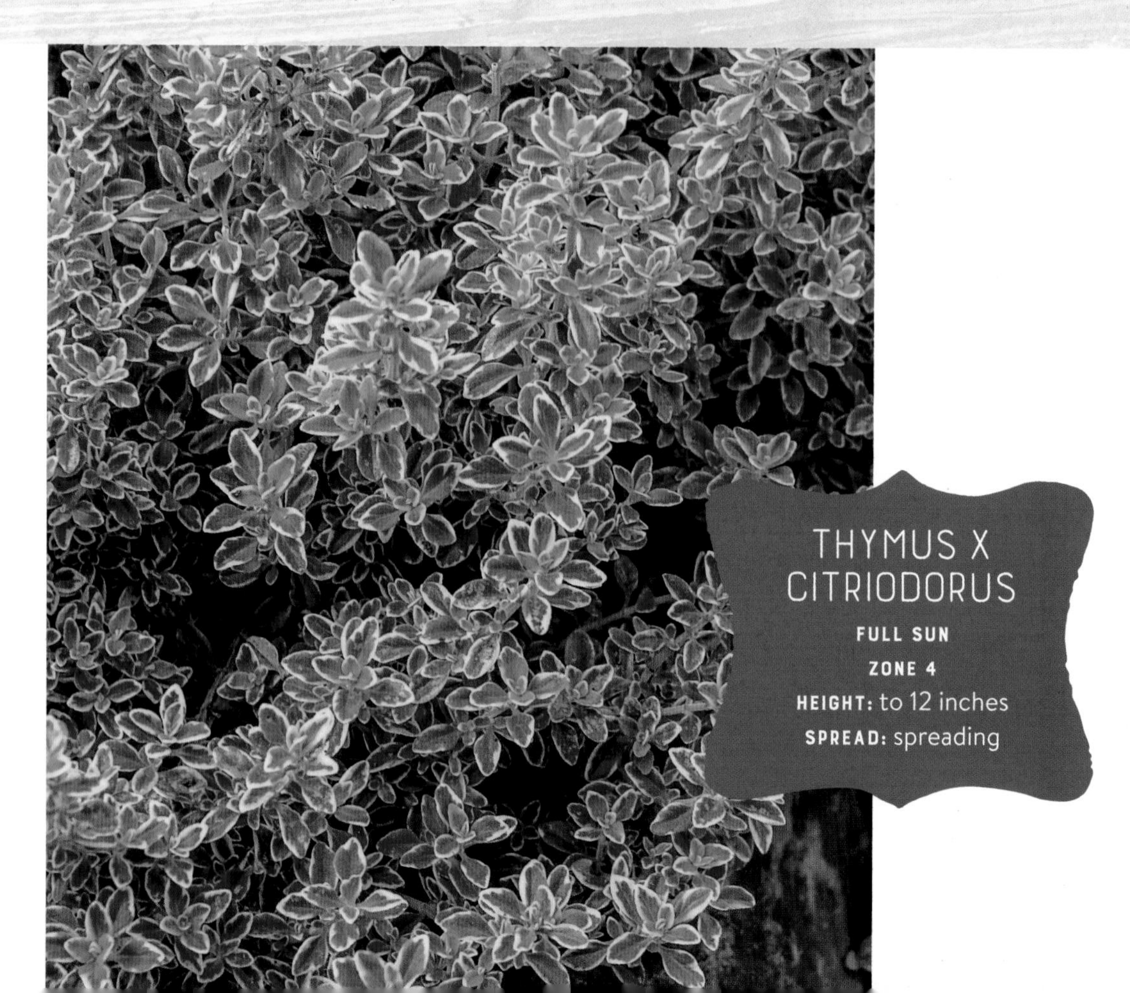

THYMUS X CITRIODORUS

FULL SUN

ZONE 4

HEIGHT: to 12 inches

SPREAD: spreading

ADAM'S NEEDLE

how to grow

Loam-based commercial soil mix amended with coarse sand for improved drainage. Tolerates winter cold, summer heat, and wind. Tolerates being root-bound and lasts many years in the same pot. Established plants form offsets at the base that can be removed and transplanted. Only care required is the removal of old flower stalks and dead leaves. Move to shelter or unheated garage in bad northern winters.

Spreads slowly to make a wide patch with many rosettes of sword-shaped leaves 2 to 3 feet long. The evergreen leaves have sharp tips and curly fibers along the edges. The tall branched stalks of large white flowers are very showy in June. 'Color Guard' shown here.

YUCCA FILAMENTOSA

FULL OR PART SUN

ZONE 5

HEIGHT: 2–3 feet (foliage); 5–6 feet (flowers)

SPREAD: 5–6 feet

LILY-OF-THE-NILE

how to grow

Tolerates heat. Loam-based commercial soil mix. Use a plastic pot or wooden container—expanding roots will break a clay pot. Ordinary watering, but tolerates drought and recovers from drying out. Feed through the summer to encourage bloom; remove faded stalks. Does well when pot-bound, but you can divide when very crowded. In cold climates, overwinter in basement; keep barely moist or stop watering. Resume watering a month before last frost and move to a sunny window.

Beautiful spheres of blue flowers on tall slender stems rise above substantial clumps of broad, arching, evergreen leaves.

AGAPANTHUS ORIENTALIS

PART OR FULL SUN

ZONE 8

HEIGHT: to 5 feet

SPREAD: 2 feet

CALADIUM

how to grow

Amend commercial loam-based soil mix with organic material such as manure, compost, or leaf mold to increase moisture retention. Plant one tuber per 8-inch pot; three for a 14-inch pot. Position tubers bumpy side up in pots indoors and put them in a warm place for a few weeks to develop roots, then move them outdoors when night temperatures reach 55°F—tubers will not root until the soil is about 65°F. Place in a spot protected from wind. Needs constant water when in active growth. Feed with high-nitrogen fertilizer. Stop watering and let leaves die down (or freeze down) in fall, then dig tubers, brush off loose soil, and let them dry for a week in a warm place before burying them in a box of vermiculite or sawdust. Store at 50°–60°F for the winter.

The large (up to 12-inch-long) arrowhead-shaped leaves have a delicate papery texture and come in solid, mottled, or spotted patterns of crimson, rose, pink, pale green, and translucent white. 'Fanny Munson' shown here.

CALADIUM X HORTULANUM

PART SUN TO SHADE

ALL ZONES

HEIGHT: 1–3 feet

SPREAD: 2 feet

CANNA

how to grow

Tolerates heat. Loam-based commercial soil mix. Large pot—at least 12 inches by 14 inches. Plant one clump per pot. Plants prefer steady moisture but tolerate some dryness. Remove faded flowers for neatness and prolonged bloom.

In Zone 8 or warmer, plant rhizomes in spring and divide every few years. In Zone 7 or colder, start rhizomes in pots indoors, a month before last frost, and put them in a warm place to start growing roots. Move them outdoors when night temperatures are above 50°F. When frost kills tops in fall, dig up rhizomes and dry them for a few days before storing them in a box of damp organic matter for the winter. Divide rhizomes in spring before repotting.

Easy to grow in large containers, cannas have big flowers in bright red, orange, salmon, pink, yellow, or white and bloom from early summer to fall.

CANNA HYBRIDS

FULL OR PART SUN
ZONE 8
HEIGHT: 2–6 feet
SPREAD: 2–3 feet

CLIVIA, KAFFIR LILY

how to grow

Loam-based commercial soil mix, well drained and enriched with organic matter. Young plants will bloom in 6-inch pots. Repot only when plant threatens to break the container or push itself out of its soil; a 12-inch pot will hold a mature clump for many years. Keep soil moist; can survive an occasional dry spell. Immediately after flowering and through the summer, give plenty of water, light, and liquid fertilizer. In fall, move to cool spot (50°F) indoors and let soil almost dry out. In late winter, when flower spikes begin to elongate, provide more light, water, and heat.

A handsome evergreen perennial, clivia has a thick rootstock that produces broad, strap-shaped dark green leaves. In late winter or early spring, dense, rounded clusters of lilylike flowers rise on stout 2-foot stems.

CLIVIA MINIATA

SUN TO SHADE

ZONE 9

HEIGHT: to 2 feet

SPREAD: to 3 feet

CROCOSMIA, MONTBRETIA

how to grow

Loam-based commercial soil mix; add coarse sand for better drainage. In spring, plant three or four corms about 4 inches deep in a large clay pot, 12 inches high and wide. Feed regularly throughout the summer. Divide after several years when clump gets crowded. Overwinter in cold frame or cold basement, or lift bulbs in fall and store indoors like gladioli. A well-grown pot of crocosmia is a sight to behold.

Makes wonderful long sprays of long-lasting, clear bright red flowers in summer, excellent as cut flowers.

CROCOSMIA 'LUCIFER'

FULL OR PART SUN

ZONE 5

HEIGHT: 3 feet

SPREAD: 1 foot

DUTCH CROCUS, COMMON CROCUS

how to grow

Loam-based commercial soil mix; for better drainage, add coarse sand. Plant 1 inch deep in shallow pots or wooden boxes; position corms almost touching for best display. Chill for 8 to 12 weeks. Keep soil moist while chilling and during bloom. Fertilize as new shoots show and again after flowering to restore energy. Allow leaves to ripen naturally after flowering, then dry corms and pot again in fall.

These are the most commonly grown crocuses, and a cheerful pot of them provides welcome late-winter or early-spring bloom. Flowers withstand frost, and they open in the sun and close at night or on cloudy days. 'Jeanne d'Arc' shown here.

CROCUS VERNUS

FULL OR PART SUN

ZONE 5

HEIGHT: 4–8 inches

SPREAD: 6 inches

FLORIST'S CYCLAMEN

how to grow

Loam-based commercial soil mix amended with coarse sand so it is moisture-retentive and well drained. Place tubers just below soil surface, one to a 6-inch pot, three to a 12-inch pot. Prefers to be slightly moist during active growth but is stressed by drought and doesn't like wet feet. Fertilize once a month to ensure continued bloom. Remove faded flowers and leaves. In summer, after corms go dormant, store pots on their side in a cool, dark place and watch out for mice because it's a favorite food. Never water until they show signs of sprouting. Undisturbed plants will gradually multiply. When repotting is necessary, do it as they resprout in autumn.

Eye-catching clumps of silver-mottled, heart-shaped leaves are topped by graceful flowers with upright petals in pink, red, magenta, or white, marked with a darker "eye" that faces downward.

CYCLAMEN PERSICUM

PART SUN TO SHADE

ZONE 9

HEIGHT: 6–12 inches

SPREAD: 6–14 inches

GLORIOSA LILY

how to grow

Loam-based commercial soil mix amended with organic matter to retain moisture. For maximum show, plant several tubers 3 inches deep in a 12-inch-by-12-inch pot; set out after danger of frost is past. Provide support in or next to pot—a trellis, strings, or brushy sticks. Keep moist and protect from hot, drying winds. Fertilize before and during bloom. Vines will turn yellow about 2 months after flowering, or when frost strikes. Carefully dig tubers, remove soil and old stalks and roots, and pack them in dry organic matter or crumpled paper. Store in cool room over winter.

Grown as an annual. Greenish yellow buds open into brilliant crimson flowers that age to a rich dark red.

GLORIOSA SUPERBA

FULL OR PART SUN

ALL ZONES

HEIGHT: 4–6 feet

SPREAD: depends on support

HYACINTH

how to grow

Loam-based commercial soil mix. Plant tips slightly below soil level and close together (almost touching) in fall. Provide 12 to 14 weeks of chilling. Bulbs may rot if soil is wet. Feed before, during, and after bloom. You can set bulbs in garden later, but for best display, buy new bulbs each fall.

Each bulb makes one spike with dozens of single or double flowers in pink, blue, lavender, rose, yellow, or white; bees love them. Leaves appear with the flowers and remain for 2 to 3 months. 'Blue Jacket' shown here.

HYACINTHUS ORIENTALIS

FULL OR PART SUN

ZONE 5

HEIGHT: 6–10 inches

SPREAD: 6 inches

RETICULATED IRIS

how to grow

Loam-based commercial soil mix. Tolerates hot, dry summers (dormant then). In fall, plant bulbs 1 inch deep and 2 inches apart in shallow container. In warm climates, keep cool over winter. In cold climates, mulch containers in cold frame or store in cold basement or shed. To force early bloom, bring into the house in late winter and place in a cool spot. Or leave them outside and wait for later bloom. Feed after they bloom, then let plants dry out. Remove yellowed leaves and store in pots or organic matter until fall.

The short-stalked flowers open in early spring, along with crocuses, snowdrops, and hellebores. They have a delicious grapelike scent. Individual blossoms are fleeting, but a large group lasts a few weeks.

IRIS RETICULATA

FULL SUN

ZONE 3

HEIGHT: 4 inches (flowers); 18 inches (foliage)

SPREAD: 2–3 inches

LILY

how to grow

Lilies tolerate summer heat if given thick mulch, regular deep watering, and afternoon shade. Use top-quality potting soil amended with coarse sand to improve drainage. To keep the soil cool in summer, underplant with spreading annuals such as sweet alyssum or lobelia. (Most shallow-rooted annuals make ideal companions.)

Plant the bulbs two to three times as deep as their diameter. Space the bulbs about 4 to 6 inches apart, and plant groups of three or five for the best show. Lilies can be left in the pots in autumn if they are stored in a cold frame, cellar, or trench in the garden. If not, remove them from the pots and store in slightly moist organic matter or wood shavings in a dark, cool spot indoors.

The flowers are typically 4 to 6 inches wide and face up, out, or down. Colors include white, yellow, orange, pink, lavender, and red.

LILIUM ASIATIC HYBRIDS

FULL OR PART SUN

ZONE 4

HEIGHT: 2–6 feet

SPREAD: 1 foot

LILY

how to grow

See opposite page for how to grow.

Lilies are rarely dormant, although they may look that way. So always be careful when handling or planting these bulbs.

And after blooming, those Easter lilies that everyone has on show during Holy Week can be moved to pots or a warm spot in the garden and will bloom the following year. Remember, it was the Greeks who thought these flowers were created from the milk of the mother of the gods, so they eventually became a Christian symbol.

The last lilies to flower in late summer, these generally have flat flowers, 6 to 8 inches or more in width, with recurved petals.

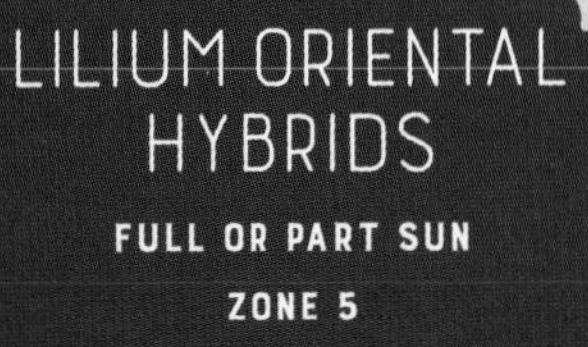

GRAPE HYACINTH

how to grow

Loam-based commercial soil mix. Use pots 8 inches wide or larger. Plant in fall, 1 inch deep, almost touching adjacent bulbs. Chill between 30°F and 40°F for 10 to 16 weeks in garage or cellar. Move when shoots are 2 inches or more tall. Water and feed until plants go dormant in summer, then store pots, unwatered, or transplant into the garden. If you keep them in the pot, top-dress every 1 or 2 years with compost or organic fertilizer. Divide when clumps get crowded.

Each bulb produces one to three stalks topped with twenty to forty closely packed, drooping, urn-shaped flowers.

MUSCARI ARMENIACUM

FULL OR PART SUN

ZONE 4

HEIGHT: 6–8 inches

SPREAD: 6 inches

DAFFODIL

how to grow

Loam-based commercial soil mix amended with coarse sand to improve drainage. Plant bulbs in fall, positioning the tips just below the soil surface. For best display, plant as many as will fit in the pot, just barely touching each other. Keep moist but not too wet. Move them to a protected area such as a porch or garage when temperatures drop below freezing. Set outside in early spring.

Resist the urge to trim off the leaves after the flowers have faded. Let them mature and die back naturally; they feed the bulb and provide for the following year's flowers.

If you leave bulbs in the same container for a few years, you may need to divide large clumps just as you would in the garden. Dig clumps when the leaves start to yellow, shake the soil off the roots, separate the bulbs, and replant them promptly. If you wait until the leaves die down completely, separate the bulbs and spread them to dry in a shady place, then remove the withered leaves and roots. Store the bulbs in mesh bags in a cool, dry shed or cellar with good air circulation until it's time to repot them in fall.

Flowers are borne on leafless stalks, singly or in small clusters. Many kinds are fragrant. All make excellent cut flowers.

NARCISSUS

FULL OR PART SUN

ZONE 4

HEIGHT: 6–20 inches

SPREAD: 4–8 inches

OXALIS

how to grow

Loam-based commercial soil mix. Plant several tubers in a 6-inch pot, or one each in 2¼-inch pots. Start them indoors 6 weeks before last frost, and keep at 60°F or warmer for good sprouting. Keep moist. Remove spent flower stalks. Let plants go dormant in fall or early winter, then store tubers in pots, or remove from pots and store in organic material such as wood chips in cool, dark place. Divide tubers in spring if necessary.

Clumps of striking four-petaled leaves, some with dark markings or a deep bronze color, are spangled with airy sprays of tiny five-petaled flowers on leafless stems held above the foliage.

OXALIS SPP.
FULL OR PART SUN
ZONE 7
HEIGHT: 6–10 inches
SPREAD: 6–10 inches

PERSIAN BUTTERCUP

how to grow

Loam-based commercial soil mix amended with coarse sand for improved drainage. In mild-winter climates, plant tubers in late fall for early-spring bloom; in cold-winter, hot-summer climates, start tubers indoors and set out after last frost. (Plants need considerable time to bloom, and an early onset of hot weather ends flowering.) Set tubers closely in containers and cover with 1 to 2 inches of soil. Keep soil moist. After bloom, let foliage ripen, then dry out pots, lift tubers, and store for the next planting cycle.

Stems with fresh green foliage carry many full-petaled double flowers in cream, yellow, orange, pink, or white; many are bicolored or have picotee edges.

RANUNCULUS ASIATICUS

FULL SUN

ZONE 8

HEIGHT: 18 inches

SPREAD: 18 inches

GARDEN TULIPS

how to grow

Soilless or loam-based commercial soil mix. Short tulips will thrive in shallow "bulb pans." Tall ones need tall pots for visual scale and to keep them from blowing over. In fall, plant bulbs so they nearly touch, cover with 1 inch or so of soil, then store planted pots in a cool place in the shade. In mild-winter areas, cover pots with mulch to delay top growth until roots have formed. In very mild regions, bulbs must be refrigerated for 6 to 8 weeks to give them an artificial "winter" or else they will not bloom. (A similar treatment is used to force potted bulbs for indoor bloom.) After flowering, continue watering for the several weeks it takes the foliage to mature. When leaves have faded, turn the bulbs out of the pots and store bulbs in a cool, dry place until fall.

The flowers are held singly on long stiff stalks (good for cutting) and come in all shades of red, orange, yellow, pink, purple, white, bicolor, and multicolor. Some kinds have a pleasant fragrance.

TULIPA

FULL SUN

ZONE 4

HEIGHT: 6–24 inches

SPREAD: 6–12 inches

BOUGAINVILLEA

how to grow

Loam-based commercial soil mix; good drainage is important. Plants tolerate occasional drying out, which seems to promote more abundant flowering. Be very careful not to disrupt the brittle roots when repotting. Young plants are very tender, but older plants can survive a light frost. Prune away damaged wood in spring, and new growth will soon replace it. Prune heavily in spring to maintain shape. Protect shrubby forms from wind by providing a strong stake. In cold climates, bring pots into a cool, bright room for the winter, and water just enough to keep the leaves from wilting.

There are dozens of cultivars in colors ranging from red, orange, pink, and purple to yellow and white, including double-flowered and variegated-leaf forms.

BOUGAINVILLEA HYBRIDS

FULL SUN OR LIGHT SHADE

ZONE 10 OR 9

HEIGHT: to 20 feet

SPREAD: to 20 feet

CLEMATIS

how to grow

Loam-based commercial soil mix; must drain well. Keep soil moist. Feed with slow-release or soluble fertilizer; stop fertilizing after late summer. Pot should be at least 1 foot wide by 18 inches deep. Wood, stone, or clay pots are ideal; raise off ground on bricks to enhance drainage and aeration. Overwinter in frost-free spot.

Pruning is important, but the timing depends on whether plants bloom on new or old shoots. If you're not certain which type your plant is when you purchase it, observe its growth and flowering the first year to find out. Those that bloom on new growth should be pruned hard, cut back to within 8 inches in earliest spring when the leaf buds begin to expand. Provide support immediately for the new shoots, which are brittle and break easily in the wind. Those that bloom on old shoots in spring and on new shoots in summer are pruned later. Remove only dead or damaged shoots in very early spring; do the main pruning-back immediately after bloom in spring.

Outstanding in bloom, hybrid clematis have flat blossoms 3 to 8 inches wide, with four to eight or more large sepals in shades from white and pink to rich red, purple, and blue.

CLEMATIS HYBRIDS

FULL OR PART SUN

ZONE 5

HEIGHT: to 15 feet

SPREAD: varies

ENGLISH IVY

how to grow

Tolerates heat. Soilless or loam-based commercial soil mix. Most kinds are happy forever in 4-inch pots; those trained as standards or pyramids may need bigger pots. Set plants deeply, removing a few lower leaves and covering that part of the stem, to encourage deep rooting. Feed lightly and often; water freely when plant is growing rapidly. Pinch to promote bushiness. Once established, prune as needed to control spread. Train on a wire frame for topiary; stake and thin out lower growth to make a standard. Requires little water in winter; bring indoors in cold areas. Be patient if top dies in winter; plant may come back from roots.

There are hundreds of cultivars, varying in leaf shape and size, coloring and variegation, vigor, and hardiness. Use the fine-leaved or variegated forms in hanging pots, window boxes, or trained as standards or topiaries. There are compact, bushy forms, too.

HEDERA HELIX

SUN TO SHADE

ZONE 6 OR 5

HEIGHT: 6 inches to 6 feet

SPREAD: 6 inches to 6 feet

MORNING GLORY

how to grow

Tolerates heat. Loam-based commercial soil mix. Can tolerate some dryness but becomes more susceptible to spider mites if too dry. Soak seeds overnight before planting. Seedlings transplant poorly, so start seeds in peat pots or directly in display pot. Set outside after danger of frost is past. Provide support immediately.

The funnel-shaped flowers, up to 5 inches wide, open in the morning and last just one day. Flowers can be blue, lavender, pink, red, or white, often with contrasting markings like five-pointed stars.

IPOMOEA PURPUREA

FULL SUN

ALL ZONES

HEIGHT: to 15 feet

SPREAD: 3–6 feet

GOLDFLAME HONEYSUCKLE

how to grow

Tolerates shade but doesn't bloom much. Loam-based commercial soil mix amended with coarse sand to improve drainage. Start in a large pot (12 to 14 inches); could eventually be moved to a half-barrel. Tolerates hot weather; give it water if it wilts. Feed with slow-release fertilizer in spring; supplement with soluble fertilizer while flower buds are developing. Cut back hard in late winter. Store dormant plant in unheated garage over winter.

A lovely vine with smooth, firm, blue-green leaves, clusters of slender 1-inch flowers that are carmine outside and yellow inside, fading to pink as they age.

LONICERA X HECKROTTII

FULL OR PART SUN

ZONE 5 OR 4

HEIGHT: 10–20 feet

SPREAD: 10–20 feet

PASSIONVINE, PASSIONFLOWER

how to grow

Loam-based commercial soil mix. Needs generous room for roots. Use one plant per large pot; space every 2 to 3 feet in planter. Don't let it dry out. Feed weekly. Prune to encourage branching, and provide support for tendrils to grasp. Allow plenty of space—this vine gets big fast. In winter, cut back and move indoors in sunny spot, or grow as annual from root cuttings.

A rambunctious vine with unbelievably intricate flowers, 3 to 4 inches wide, in shades of purple or white. Very fragrant and blooms all summer. The Passion of its name refers to the Passion of Christ because so many parts of the blossom, not to mention the plant's coiled vines, refer to symbols found in the Crucifixion.

PASSIFLORA X ALATOCAERULEA

FULL SUN

ZONE 8 OR 7

HEIGHT: 10–12 feet

SPREAD: 10–12 feet

BLACK-EYED SUSAN VINE

how to grow

Loam-based commercial soil mix. Start seeds indoors in peat pots 6 to 8 weeks before last frost; transplant in a pot at the base of shrubs or a trellis. Needs constant moisture; best grown where summers are warm and moist—dislikes cool temperatures and arid climates.

This twining climber has toothed oval leaves and flat, five-petaled flowers with a dark "eye" and orange-yellow, buff, apricot, even white petals.

THUNBERGIA ALATA

FULL OR PART SUN

ALL ZONES

HEIGHT: 3–8 feet

SPREAD: 3–6 feet

JAPANESE MAPLE

how to grow

When soil is kept moist, Japanese maples tolerate heat yet still resent drying winds. Use a loam-based commercial soil mix. To prevent leaf burn, never use water that is tainted with alkalines or salt. Every few months during active growth, use a weak fertilizer. When a plant reaches a desired size, to keep it in the same pot you can root-prune, then add fresh soil. In winter climates where the pots and soil freeze one day, then melt the next, to prevent root damage store maples in a cool place or dig a trench and bury the pots and mulch heavily for frost protection. Then in late winter or early spring, bring them back to your container garden.

Overlapping tiers of arching branches form a wide, rounded crown. The foliage is outstanding in summer and fall, and the bark and branching are attractive in winter.

ACER PALMATUM

SUN TO SHADE

ZONE 6 OR 5

HEIGHT: to 10 feet

SPREAD: often wider than tall

JAPANESE BARBERRY

how to grow

Soilless commercial mix. Start in a 12- to 14-inch pot; eventually could be planted in a tub. Feed with slow-release fertilizer in spring. Very hardy to cold but weakened by extremely hot summers. Remove dead stems and prune to shape after flowering. Overwinter outdoors, or store in cold location.

Has dense thorny stems, small teardrop-shaped leaves, and bright red berries in fall.

BERBERIS THUNBERGII

FULL SUN

ZONE 4

HEIGHT: to 6 feet

SPREAD: to 6 feet

BUTTERFLY BUSH

how to grow

Loam-based commercial soil mix; good drainage is essential. Tolerates dryness. Repot every 1 to 2 years. Prune buddleias in containers to the ground in late winter to force a fountain of fresh shoots. They can grow 5 feet tall in a season.

A trouble-free shrub with long clusters of fragrant flowers at the tip of every arching branch. Blooms on new wood from midsummer to fall. 'Miss Molly' shown here.

BUDDLEIA DAVIDII

FULL SUN

ZONE 5

HEIGHT: to 10 feet but usually less

SPREAD: to 10 feet

BLUEBEARD, BLUE SPIREA

how to grow

Tolerates heat. Loam-based commercial soil mix plus added grit to improve drainage. Recovers from drying out. One plant per 14- to 16-inch pot. Feed with slow-release fertilizer in spring; supplement during summer with soluble fertilizer. Cut back drastically to a woody base in spring to promote shapely new growth. Overwinter dormant plant in unheated garage; keep soil dry.

New spring shoots have neatly spaced pairs of downy gray leaves. Fluffy clusters of lavender-blue flowers tip each shoot in August and September and attract butterflies.

CARYOPTERIS X CLANDONENSIS

FULL SUN

ZONE 6 OR 5

HEIGHT: 2–3 feet

SPREAD: 2–3 feet

HARRY LAUDER'S WALKING STICK

how to grow

Loam-based commercial soil mix; must be well drained. Plant in a large pot or tub, where it will stay for years. These plants are almost always propagated by grafting, but the understock inevitably suckers vigorously, making corrective pruning an annual ritual. Cut all straight shoots back to the base. You can prune to shape at any time, though spring is best.

Named for a famous Scottish entertainer, these shrubs are most interesting in winter. Like Harry's famous walking stick, the plant's contorted branches twist into incredible and irregular spirals with shiny brown bark. In late winter and early spring these shrubs bloom with 3-inch-long male catkins that dangle like ornaments to celebrate the coming end of winter.

CORYLUS AVELLANA 'CONTORTA'

FULL OR PART SUN

ZONE 4

HEIGHT: 7–8 feet

SPREAD: 5–6 feet

DAPHNE

how to grow

Loam-based commercial soil mix amended with organic matter and coarse sand to improve drainage. Tolerates hot weather. Buy container-grown plant and repot in display pot; roots resent disturbance. Repotting is not needed for many years. Needs no pruning beyond the removal of damaged shoots. Slow growing but free of pests or diseases if drainage is good.

Forms a dense, compact, mounded shrub with neat, small, oval leaves. A profusion of small, starry pale pink flowers covers the plant for several weeks in late spring. They are deliciously fragrant, and one plant perfumes the entire garden. 'Carol Mackie' shown here.

DAPHNE X BURKWOODII

FULL SUN OR PART SHADE

ZONE 4

HEIGHT: 3–4 feet

SPREAD: 3–4 feet

COMMON FIG

how to grow

Loam-based commercial soil mix. Pot or tub should be as large as you can lift or otherwise move. Recovers from drying out; don't overwater. Prune to control size and shape, removing weak or crossed limbs. Pinching early in season promotes branching, but eliminates early fruit crop. Protect fruit from birds. North of Zone 8, store above freezing. Plants—tub and all—can be buried under soil and straw, or left upright and wrapped in old blankets and straw. Watch out for the milky sap—it stains hands and clothing.

A distinctive shrub or tree, often multi-trunked, with large, coarse lobed leaves on thick stems. Makes a bold, interesting specimen. The tiny flowers develop into sweet, tasty figs.

FICUS CARICA

FULL SUN

ZONE 8 OR 7

HEIGHT: 5–6 feet

SPREAD: 2–3 feet

HYDRANGEA

how to grow

Tolerates heat. Loam-based commercial soil mix amended with plenty of organic matter and coarse sand for improved drainage. Use aluminum sulfate to acidify soil for blue flowers and lime to produce red flowers. Needs constant moisture; easily dries out, so monitor soil moisture closely. Blooms on previous season's growth. While plant is dormant, remove stems that have already flowered. Further thinning will promote larger flower clusters. Hydrangeas are long-lived and trouble-free.

Showy rounded clusters of white, pink, red, or blue flowers bloom in summer and fall. The big leaves have a thick texture and shiny green color.

HYDRANGEA MACROPHYLLA

FULL OR PART SUN

ZONE 6

HEIGHT: 4–8 feet

SPREAD: 6–10 feet

CRAPE MYRTLE

how to grow

Loam-based commercial soil mix amended with coarse sand to improve drainage. Thrives in hot weather and recovers from dryness. Blooms on new growth; if shoots freeze back in a severe winter, it will recover the same year. Prune hard in spring to control growth and to encourage larger flowers. Remove suckers to expose and feature the trunks.

The small flowers in large clusters have a texture like crepe paper and come in many shades of pink, rosy red, purple, or white. Leaves are smooth ovals, 2 to 4 inches long, sometimes turning red, orange, or purplish in fall.

LAGERSTROEMIA INDICA

FULL OR PART SUN

ZONE 7

HEIGHT: to 25 feet

SPREAD: to 10 feet

MINIATURE ROSES

how to grow

Use a loam-based commercial soil mix amended with lots of organic matter and coarse sand for drainage. Never let them dry out, and avoid wetting the leaves when watering. During active growth, feed every 7 to 10 days with soluble fertilizer.

Roses need careful pruning to establish the shape of the bush, to remove old or damaged shoots, and to promote vigorous growth and abundant flowering. When and how to prune varies among the different groups; in general, prune before the plant begins growth in spring, and prune plants in containers harder than you would those in the ground.

Overwinter as necessary in a frost-free location. Outdoors in marginal areas, apply a thick mulch for insulation.

Short plants with thin canes, closely spaced small leaves, and perfect little buds and flowers. There are dozens of cultivars in all colors.

ROSA MINIATURE ROSES

FULL SUN

ZONES VARY

HEIGHT: varies

SPREAD: varies

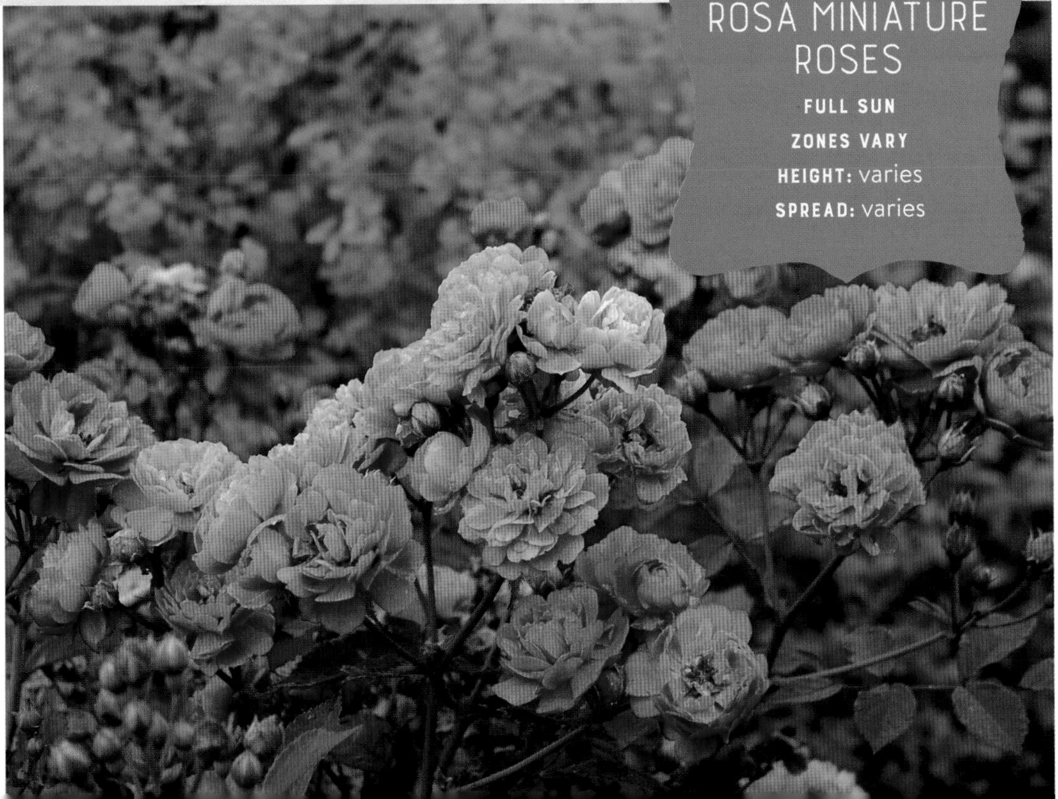

RED ELDERBERRY

how to grow

Loam-based commercial soil mix. Mature plant may need a tub or whiskey barrel. Needs constant moisture. Prune to shape during growing season; cut back hard in late winter to control size of plant and to encourage branching. Overwinter in unheated garage if necessary.

The cultivars of this species offer a rounded bush of very attractive foliage with 5- to 6-inch panicles of white flowers in spring and red fruits in summer. 'Plumosa Aurea' shown here.

SAMBUCUS RACEMOSA

FULL OR PART SUN

ZONE 4

HEIGHT: 3–6 feet

SPREAD: 3–6 feet

KOREAN SPICE VIBURNUM

how to grow

Loam-based commercial soil mix. Most require large containers; stone, clay, or wooden containers are best. Never allow to dry out—a thick organic mulch helps keep the roots cool and moist. Feed with slow-release fertilizer. Prune after flowering to control size, although this removes the fruits. Renew established plants by cutting old and weak stems to the ground in early spring. Protect during the winter, particularly the evergreens.

Extremely fragrant white flowers, which form dome-shaped clusters 2 to 3 inches wide in April, followed by clusters of black fruit. Leaves are dull green in summer, sometimes turning reddish in fall.

VIBURNUM CARLESII 'COMPACTUM'

FULL OR PART SUN

ZONE 4

HEIGHT: 3 feet

SPREAD: 3 feet

CHASTE TREE, PEPPERBUSH

how to grow

Thrives in hot weather. Loam-based commercial soil mix. Start in a 20-inch pot; can eventually be moved to a tub. Recovers from drying out. Prune in spring to control size. Store in unheated garage over winter.

Leaves are dark green above and gray-green or silver below and release a spicy fragrance when crushed. Clustered 4- to 10-inch spikes of small lilac or lavender flowers bloom on the new growth from midsummer through fall and attract butterflies.

VITEX AGNUS-CASTUS

FULL SUN

ZONE 7

HEIGHT: 3–6 feet

SPREAD: 3–6 feet

AGAVE

how to grow

Loam-based commercial soil mix (you might add sand to weigh down the container to keep plant from tipping). Tolerates dryness. Protect from severe frost. Confining to container will slow plants' growth, making them unlikely to reach flowering size. Eventually they may outgrow your space.

Makes a statuesque rosette of fleshy, pale jade leaves, becoming a natural sculpture for dry landscapes or seaside gardens.

AGAVE ATTENUATA

FULL SUN OR PART SHADE

ZONE 9

HEIGHT: 5 feet

SPREAD: 5 feet

LITTLELEAF BOX

how to grow

Loam-based commercial soil mix; must be well drained. Start in a 12- to 14-inch pot; at maturity may need a 20- to 22-inch pot or tub. Boxwoods have shallow roots that need special attention. Water regularly; a mulch may help keep them from drying out, but leave an open space around the trunk to prevent stem rot. Feed with slow-release fertilizer and occasional soluble fertilizer supplement during active growth. Prune to shape after new growth emerges in spring. Overwinter out of strong winds; keep soil on the dry side.

The dense branching and closely set, glossy, fine-textured foliage make this an ideal shrub for containers, and it can be sheared into formal shapes or topiary.

BUXUS MICROPHYLLA

FULL OR PART SUN

ZONE 5

HEIGHT: to 4 feet

SPREAD: to 4 feet

LEMON BOTTLEBRUSH

how to grow

Loam-based commercial soil mix. Tolerates heat and recovers from drying out. Plant in a deep, 10- to 16-inch pot; an 8- to 10-inch pot will do for dwarf forms. May need iron supplement if water contains sodium or calcium. To train a tree, provide a stake and remove lower branches until a head is formed. Prune just behind spent blooms to limit size. Move indoors over winter in cold climates.

A mounded shrub with arching branches that can be trained as a small tree. The bright red flowers make 6-inch "bottlebrushes" near the ends of the branches; flushes of bloom appear sporadically in all seasons and attract hummingbirds.

CALLISTEMON CITRINUS

FULL SUN

ZONE 9

HEIGHT: 4–5 feet

SPREAD: 4–5 feet

CAMELLIA

how to grow

Needs well-drained, acidic potting soil amended with plenty of organic matter. Use an acid-type fertilizer after bloom. Keep soil moist and cool; mulch helps. With root pruning, can grow in a 12-inch pot; a 2-foot box or tub allows plants to grow larger. Repot just before, during, or after bloom. Pinch runaway shoots; cut back to dormant growth buds (slight swellings on stems) to encourage bushy growth. In marginal areas, overwinter in cool (40°F) greenhouse.

The oval dark green leaves of gardenias are glossy and leathery. Usually, in late winter or early spring, plump round flower buds at the ends of the branches open into showy single or double flowers in white, shades of pink, or red; the cultivar 'C. M. Wilson' is shown here. Unfortunately, these incredible blossoms have no fragrance but if they did, they would be one of the most popular flowers on earth.

CAMELLIA JAPONICA

PART SUN TO SHADE

ZONE 8 OR 7

HEIGHT: 5 feet

SPREAD: 3–4 feet

HINOKI CYPRESS

how to grow

Loam-based commercial soil mix. Smallest forms can fit in 6-inch pots; larger in pots or boxes up to 16 inches. Keep soil moist. Underpotting will restrict growth, as will root pruning. Feed bonsai and plants in small pots frequently; larger plants can be fed in early spring and early summer, or use a slow-release fertilizer. Repot only when plant shows signs of stress—roots on surface of soil, drying out too quickly, poor color. Protect from winter sun and wind, which can discolor or scorch the foliage. Keep root mass from freezing solid.

The Hinoki cypress's rich emerald green color and the soft texture of the flattened sprays of tiny rounded scales are appealing. The dwarf forms make excellent patio plants.

CHAMAECYPARIS OBTUSA AND ITS CULTIVARS

FULL OR PART SUN

ZONE 5

HEIGHT: 2–6 feet (dwarf forms)

SPREAD: 1–3 feet (dwarf forms)

SAWARA CYPRESS

how to grow

Loam-based commercial soil mix. Use 6-inch pots for the smallest ones; larger forms can go in pots up to 16 inches. Keep soil moist. Using pots that are too small will restrict growth, as will root pruning. Feed bonsai and plants in small pots frequently; feed larger plants in early spring and early summer, or use a slow-release fertilizer. Repot only when plant shows signs of stress—roots on surface of soil, drying out too quickly, poor color. Protect from winter sun and wind, which can discolor or scorch the foliage. Keep root mass from freezing solid.

'Boulevard' (shown here) makes an irregular cone, slowly reaching 10 feet or more, and has especially soft and fluffy foliage, silver-blue in summer, tinged purple in winter. Retains dead brown foliage and needs pruning for tidiness and to reveal the branch structure as it ages.

CHAMAECYPARIS PISIFERA CULTIVARS

FULL OR PART SUN

ZONE 5

HEIGHT: 1–8 feet

SPREAD: 1–5 feet

CITRUS

how to grow

Soilless or loam-based commercial soil mix. Will grow in 6- to 8-inch pots but are bigger and better in 12-inch or larger pots. Root-prune to control size. Feed frequently during growing season; may need supplemental iron and trace elements. Little pruning is required. Overwinter on a sun porch or in a cool greenhouse at temperatures above 25°F to 28°F.

Evergreen trees or shrubs, usually spiny, with glossy simple leaves, richly fragrant white or pale pink flowers, and aromatic juicy fruit. This genus includes oranges, lemons, grapefruits, limes, and other citrus fruits. Ponderosa lemon *(Citrus* x *pyriformis)* shown here. The first greenhouses were called orangeries, in a salute to these wonderful fruits.

CITRUS
FULL SUN
ZONE 9
HEIGHT: varies
SPREAD: varies

GLOSSY-LEAVED PAPER PLANT

how to grow

Loam-based commercial soil mix enriched with organic matter. Needs large container. Keep soil moist, but it will recover from drying out. Can prune hard in spring—be bold. Difficult to shape by pruning; tends to grow as it chooses.

An upright shrub with big, coarse, glossy leaves. Sometimes makes rounded clusters of tiny white flowers, followed by small dark fruits.

FATSIA JAPONICA

PART SUN TO SHADE

ZONE 7

HEIGHT: 6–10 feet

SPREAD: 6–10 feet

JAPANESE HOLLY

how to grow

Loam-based commercial soil mix amended with organic matter and coarse sand for improved drainage. Wooden containers are best; stands crowded conditions if well fed and watered. Don't allow to dry out. Needs minimal care or pruning. Grows naturally into a compact dense shrub. Overwinter in frost-free location.

The thick, leathery, dark green leaves are small ovals and the small, inconspicuous berries are black.

ILEX CRENATA

FULL OR PART SUN

ZONE 5

HEIGHT: usually under 4 feet

SPREAD: varies

SWEETBAY

how to grow

Tolerates heat. Loam-based commercial soil mix. Looks best in large formal-looking pots or boxes 14 to 16 inches wide (at plant's maturity). Recovers from drying out. Feed lightly through spring and early summer. Shape with pruning shears by snipping individual leaves or small twigs, not with hedge shears, which will mutilate foliage. Can be trained into lollipop standards or formal cones, balls, or pyramids. Bring indoors when temperatures reach mid- to low teens.

A dense evergreen with year-round unchanging good looks. The pointed oval leaves are stiff, leathery, dark green. Tight clusters of small greenish yellow flowers are inconspicuous in early spring, and shiny black fruits are more obvious in fall.

LAURUS NOBILIS

FULL SUN

ZONE 8

HEIGHT: 6 feet

SPREAD: 3 feet

HEAVENLY BAMBOO

how to grow

Tolerates heat. Soilless or loam-based commercial soil mix. Will do well for years in a 12- to 14-inch pot or box. Repot when plant appears seriously root-bound. Recovers from drying out. Prune older stems to soil level to encourage low, dense new growth; or prune all stems back to soil level if plant becomes too dense. Tops may freeze in Zones 7 and 6; cut back to live wood in spring. Thrives over winter in bright room.

Leaves are at first pastel pink or coppery, then turn light to dark green in summer and rich crimson or purple in fall and winter. Loose clusters of creamy white flowers open in early summer. Heavy sprays of shiny red berries last from fall to spring. Misnamed from the beginning, these small shrubs have nothing to do with the bamboo family, which are grasses, not flowering plants.

NANDINA DOMESTICA

SUN TO SHADE

ZONES 7 AND 6

HEIGHT: 4–5 feet

SPREAD: 2 feet

DWARF ALBERTA SPRUCE

how to grow

Loam-based commercial soil mix amended with organic matter for increased moisture retention. Wooden or clay containers will help prevent excessive heating of soil.

Protect root zone with a layer of mulch; roots are too shallow for underplanting. Don't allow to dry out. Shapes itself naturally and doesn't need much, if any, pruning. Protect shallow roots from winter cold.

It looks like a cone upholstered with slightly prickly fake fur—the small, pale green needles are densely crowded on the twigs—and it takes decades to reach 10 feet tall.

PICEA GLAUCA 'CONICA'

FULL OR PART SUN

ZONE 3

HEIGHT: to 10 feet

SPREAD: 3 feet

BLUE SPRUCE

how to grow

Loam-based commercial soil mix amended with organic matter to increase moisture retention. Use wooden or clay containers to prevent excessive heating of soil.

Protect root zone with a layer of mulch; roots are too shallow for underplanting. Don't let the plant dry out. Shapes itself naturally and needs little to no pruning. Protect shallow roots from winter cold.

A symbol of the Colorado Rockies, where its erect pyramidal shape echoes the mountain peaks. Popular in other regions for its colored foliage and rigid posture. Young trees are especially neat and formal, with tiers of horizontal branches.

PICEA PUNGENS

FULL SUN

ZONE 3

HEIGHT: varies with cultivar

SPREAD: varies with cultivar

ROSEMARY

how to grow

Tolerates heat. Loam-based commercial soil mix; add lime to make it slightly alkaline. Mature plants do nicely in 6- to 12-inch pots. Has deep roots, so a deep pot is useful, though you'll still have to root-prune. Suffers from overwatering and from drying out. Feed once every 3 weeks in spring and summer. Pinch growing tips to promote full, bushy growth. Overwinter indoors in cool (40°F and up at night), sunny room.

The gray-green needlelike leaves of Rosemary are very aromatic. Appearing in late winter to early spring, small light blue, lilac, or white flowers form on old wood and last for weeks.

ROSMARINUS OFFICINALIS

FULL SUN

ZONE 8

HEIGHT: 2–3 feet

SPREAD: 2 feet

how to grow

Loam-based commercial soil mix amended with coarse sand for good drainage, which is vital. Water regularly, though all are somewhat drought tolerant. Can stay years in one container. Prune or shear in late spring following elongation of new growth. Feed in spring with slow-release fertilizer.

Yew needles are flat and narrow, under 1 inch long, with pointed tips. Male plants produce a cloud of pollen in spring while females bear red fruits in fall, called *Taxus baccata*. Yews can exist for centuries, yet all parts of the yew, except for the flesh around the seed in the berry, are poisonous.

TAXUS CULTIVARS

SUN TO SHADE
ZONE: varies
HEIGHT: varies
SPREAD: varies

AMERICAN ARBORVITAE, EASTERN WHITE CEDAR

how to grow

Loam-based commercial soil mix amended with organic matter for moisture retention. Prune to maintain size, if necessary. The most common problem is winter storm damage. Heavy wet snows can open up the center and spread the leaders apart or leave them sprawling on the ground. Prevent this by using wire or rot-resistant twine to tie the leaders together in several places. Suffers in hot summers and, except for the mountain regions, doesn't do well across the southern United States.

The rich green foliage is quite fragrant when crushed. The tiny scalelike leaves are arranged in flat sprays that tilt in all directions.

THUJA OCCIDENTALIS

FULL SUN

ZONE 3

HEIGHT: 2–10 feet

SPREAD: varies with pruning

FRAGRANT
GARDENS

Angel's trumpet *(Brugmansia suaveolens)*

INTRODUCTION TO FRAGRANT GARDENS

In the late 1500s, Christopher Marlowe wrote the following lines for his poem "The Passionate Shepherd to His Love": "And I will make thee beds of roses / And a thousand fragrant posies."

In 1860, some 270 years later, Ralph Waldo Emerson opined in *The Conduct of Life*, "I wish that life should not be cheap, but sacred. I wish the days to be as centuries, loaded, fragrant."

The first is a declaration of love, the second a philosophy of life. Both reflect on one of mankind's five primary senses—the sense of smell.

Many idiomatic sayings are also associated with this sense, including a few that are not complimentary, for example, "It smells to high heaven"; "I am beginning to smell a rat"; and "They wrinkled their noses at the smell." For every ill smell that's recalled, however, there are dozens of proverbs, axioms, and, yes, even clichés linked to pleasant memories that usually involve flowers.

Trey Fromme, a young landscape architect lecturing at Longwood Gardens, once talked about the fragrant garden and said that we don't often use "odor or fragrance as a focal point in the garden." It's time to do so in the garden world.

I hope that this small book helps to point the way.

floral fragrances for today

FASHIONS CHANGE, and the popularity of fragrances is no exception; one generation's most popular scent is an anathema to the next. But a few classifications seem to be constant.

Burkwood osmanthus (Osmanthus x burkwoodii)

Heavy is a fragrance classification that describes those sweet-smelling flowers (and perfumes) that can be overpowering at close range. In the flower category, mock orange (*Philadelphus* spp.), tuberoses, osmanthus, some lilies, and many honeysuckles come to mind. In his 1597 herbal, the English botanist John Gerard called the mock orange "too sweet, troubling and molesting the head in a strange manner." For those with a chemical frame of mind, these scents contain benzyl acetate, indole, and methyl anthranilate. Indole, found in the excrement of animals (including humans), points to the fact that life has always been a strange mix.

When it comes to perfumes, many of the cheaper brands are best described as heavy, and discretion is often the better part of valor regarding the high-priced varieties.

One of the common names of *Gladiolus murielae* is fragrant gladiolus.

The pink members of the rugosas *(Rosa rugosa)* grow with single or double flowers and range in blossom color from deep pinks to bright pinks to those with petals of a soft, clear pink. Most are delightfully fragrant.

Aromatic represents those flowers having a spicy fragrance like the garden pink. The chemicals, among others, that conspire to create these odors include cinnamic alcohol, eugenol, and vanilla. (I can remember the marvels of taking the cap from a bottle of real vanilla and inhaling that marvelous sweet fragrance.) Many aromatic flowers, particularly nocturnal flowers, contain some of the chemicals found in the flower group classified as heavy—night-scented stock, nicotiana, many tropical orchids, heliotropes, and *Gladiolus tristis*, for instance. Surprisingly, while many of the orchids do have powerful scents, none of the plants in the aromatic group contain indole, so even if the flowers that produce these fragrances appear to be strange or even bizarre, their odor is never overpowering.

Lemon contains citral, a chemical found in oil of lemon, oil of orange, and bay leaves. Although it isn't common in the typical garden flower, lemon scent is very noticeable in magnolias, water lilies, many fragrant daylilies, and four-o'clocks.

Foxy is the term applied to the last category of flowers. This polite term refers to plants or blossoms that have a certain ferine odor, slightly musky but certainly not equal to the odor of a cave full of stegosauruses, and not potent enough to lead to the defenestration of the offending plant. When one tries to imagine the privileged haunts of the royal classes (forgetting about sties, privies, and local taverns) of most of the centuries leading up to today's age of soap and deodorant, you have some idea of just how harmless most of the plants that suffer with names including *stinking, smelly,* or *foxy* really are. Other than the leaves of a boxwood after a rain and a few tropical trees that are pollinated by bats, I can't think of any garden flower that fits this description.

garden care and maintenance

THE PLANTS DESCRIBED in this book range from those that are happy in water to those that prefer the driest of soils to those few that can survive in pure clay. To ensure the best growth and the happiest flowers, make sure you know what kind of soil your garden will provide.

Oleanders (*Nerium oleander*) are shrubs that originated in the gardens of India. They perfume the summer air with the fragrance of almonds. Remember, all parts of this plant are poisonous.

TYPES OF SOIL

As you plan a fragrance garden, check your soil for its character: Is it solid clay, rich loam, or a combination of both? Is it well drained or does the water stand in puddles even after a light rain?

Clay soils are sticky. If you roll a lump of wet backyard soil between your fingers and it forms a compact cylinder that refuses to break up, it's clay. Clay isn't all bad, as it contains valuable minerals that plants need for good growth. When dry, however, clay can be rock hard, and instead of percolating into that soil, rain or hose water simply rolls to the lowest level.

The opposite effect occurs with sandy soils: water is absorbed so quickly that the soil is often dry within hours of a heavy rain.

The best garden material is a good mix of soil and organic

matter, much like that found in the woods, where leaves fall and rot over thousands of years. Plus, of course, good drainage. Of all the factors essential to good gardening, the most important is drainage.

There are many ways to improve your impoverished soil. You can add compost from your own compost pile; seasoned manure (fresh manure is usually too strong to plant in directly, so mix it in the soil thoroughly in late fall, winter, or very early spring, and wait a few months before direct planting); leaf-litter; or bags of composted manure, which can be found at garden centers.

RAISED BEDS

If your soil is really bad and not worth the effort to improve, how about making a raised bed? Instead of digging down, mark out your area and build it up about 2 to 3 feet above the ground level using railroad ties from the lumber yard. If you are not sure whether the ties have been treated with creosote (newer ties generally are free of the chemical), be sure to ask, as it's dangerous to people and pets. Alternatively, you can build a wall of concrete blocks, fieldstone, or even bricks. Then fill the new area with your own or purchased topsoil.

If you live on the side of a hill, you can do this to build terraces and prevent the rain from washing down the slopes.

A NURSERY BED

If your garden is expanding and you wish to try new plants, especially those grown from seed, plan for a small nursery bed in your garden. It need not be large, but it should be in a protected spot, have good soil, have access to water, and be out of the way so that you aren't under pressure to consider aesthetics. Here you can raise seedling plants to maturity before planting them in the garden proper.

WATERING THE GARDEN

The traditional rule of thumb is that gardens need 1 inch of water per week. Not many of us keep rain gauges in our gardens (although we should),

A plant such as variegated sweet iris (*Iris pallida* 'Variegata') needs water weekly, or more often when heat is extreme.

and moisture needs change depending on weather conditions, soil type, plant type, and the surrounding environment. For example, there is more evaporation with high winds. Generally, if your garden gets a good soaking rain once a week, you'll be able to forget about watering. But gardens in fast-draining sandy soils may need additional water, as may gardens in hot climates. Plants summering outdoors in pots will also need to be watered daily, or perhaps twice a day, depending on the size of the pot. Shallow-rooted plants must have more water than deep-rooted varieties, and new plants require constant moisture to help establish fledgling roots. The best way to tell when the garden needs water is to stick your finger in the soil. If it feels dry a couple of inches below the surface, it's time to water.

Overhead sprinklers are the least efficient, especially in areas of high sun, high heat, and porous soil. Soaker hoses have tiny holes that release water slowly and are better than sprinklers. Drip irrigation systems are best because they deliver water directly to the root zone. Kits are available that include the necessary hose attachments. Just attach the system to a water source, install a timer if you like, and you're ready to go.

MULCH: KEEPING THE GARDEN MOIST

Each year it's more difficult to welcome the dog days of summer, because with every new July or August, the sun beats down with increased strength, baking the soil and evaporating water. A garden mulch will help to conserve water and also cut down on the growth of weeds. And a neatly applied layer of mulch often looks better between the plants than parched dirt.

Mulching helps plants such as meadowsweet *(Filipendula ulmaria)* retain its moisture, especially during bloom time from June through August.

A number of mulches are available around the country, including buckwheat hulls, chopped-up corn cobs, marble chips, pea gravel, pecan hulls, pine bark chips, pine needles, and for those in love with the smell of chocolate, cocoa husks. You can also use garden compost, hay, and leaf mold (soft leaves like maple will mat, unlike the tough leaves of oaks). Never use peat moss; when completely dry it becomes a hardened mass that sheds water like a hot griddle scatters droplets.

In addition, some people use black plastic but if you do, be sure to cover it with a less offensive material.

PROPPING THE PLANTS

Some plants grow well with stout and sturdy stems; others become top-heavy with fragrant blooms and have a habit of bending over, particularly during those sudden thunderstorms of summer. So it becomes necessary to prop them up. Here are four methods.

Pea-staking, an English invention, involves placing branches pruned from trees upright in a perennial bed early in the season. The plants grow up through the sticks and cover them with foliage. The branches should be 6 inches shorter than the leaves of the plant. We use birch, wild cherry, and maple taken from our neighboring woodlands. The name originated in the vegetable garden, where this method was used to support pea vines.

Wire plant supports, which originated in Scotland, consist of heavy concentric wire rings wrapped around three metal legs. The plants grow up through the rings.

Bamboo or reed stakes can be used to support single-stemmed plants. I gather all the stems of my eulalia grasses *(Miscanthus sinensis)* in late fall and use them with twist-ties or plastic clips.

Cat's-cradle is achieved by setting out four short corner stakes and winding green garden twine across and between.

A WORD ABOUT CLIMATE ZONES

The United States Department of Agriculture (USDA) Zone Map (see page 198) is based on average *minimum* temperatures found in various parts of the United States and Canada (the map refers only to a plant's hardiness to cold weather, not to heat or other factors like drought or humidity). Even then, the zones are only guidelines. For a more accurate idea as to the highs and lows for your area, contact your county's extension service.

Microclimates are also important. These are areas sheltered from the worst of the winter winds, areas that receive protection from the grace of being behind a small hill, places that enjoy extra warmth provided by heat leaking from a nearby warm building foundation, or a spot that gets extra sunlight even on a sunny day in winter. One of the marvelous adventures of gardening is experimenting with plant placement and succeeding with a rare plant where other gardeners have failed because they did not provide that extra measure of protection.

ANNUAL PLANTS ARE THE UNSUNG HEROES OF THE GARDEN. They will germinate, grow, flower, and seed all in one season. Many of them complete this speedy life cycle in 12 to 14 weeks. As such, annuals are the closest thing to instant gratification in the garden. And there are a number of these fast-track plants that produce marvelous fragrances. A number of tropical plants that are perennial in warmer climes are treated as annuals in northern gardens. Unless noted, all of these plants will do well in any reasonably good, well-drained garden soil, in full sun except in the Deep South, where they will welcome some noontime shade.

SOME FRAGRANT ANNUALS

The following plants can be found in most seed catalogs or garden centers; a few are available only from the smaller seed houses that specialize in more unusual plants.

Pot marigold
(Calendula officinalis)

POT MARIGOLDS *(Calendula officinalis)* were once grown not for their pungent leaves and stems and fragrant flowers but as pharmaceuticals for home healers. The flowers grow as wide as 4 inches and are available in a wide variety of colors, such as orange, apricot, cream, and bright yellow. Although the long narrow leaves are slightly clammy to the touch, the blossoms are a delight to both eye and nose. Mass them in the garden or grow them in pots, being sure to remove spent blossoms to ensure continued bloom. Start calendulas indoors six weeks before your last frost, or sow seeds directly in the garden as soon as the ground can be worked. Space dwarf varieties 8 inches apart and taller types about a foot apart.

Queen Anne's pocket melon
(Cucumis melo)

QUEEN ANNE'S POCKET MELON *(Cucumis melo)* is a small annual vine that grows no taller than 6 feet and bears 3-inch yellow flowers, followed by oval fruits that are green at first and then turn to yellow stripes on a brown background when ripe. Forget the flowers and grow this vine for the sweet perfume of the ripened fruit. It is said that good Queen Anne would carry this little melon in her reticule as she walked the rather dank palace halls, inhaling its fragrance now and then to be relieved from the various castle odors. For August fruit, start the seeds directly outdoors as soon as frost has passed. For an early start, you can plant seeds in 3-inch peat pots about 4 weeks before the last frost, using three seeds per pot and discarding the weaker two seedlings. A string trellis is quite adequate to hold the vine.

The thorn apple family of plants contains two species of annuals; the first is called **ANGEL'S TRUMPET** *(Datura metel)*. The tall, rambling plants bear many foot-long trumpet-shaped cream-colored to pure white flowers, often 8 inches long and intensely fragrant. The plant is sometimes called *D. meteloides* when the flowers have a lavender tinge. The second plant is ***D. stramonium,*** a pantropic weed with ill-smelling foliage and spiny seedpods, yet beautiful, sweet-smelling white flowers, almost like the regular angel's trumpet. Try to grow the first and be very careful of the second. All are poisonous!

Angel's trumpet
(Datura metel)

Start seeds 6 weeks before the last frost, using 3-inch peat pots with two seeds per pot. Remove the smaller seedling. Daturas will flower in 14 weeks from seed and do well in pots on a terrace. If the soil is too rich, you will get large, healthy leaves and fewer flowers. Provide some shade on hot afternoons.

Sweet William
(Dianthus barbatus)

SWEET WILLIAM *(Dianthus barbatus)* is a common pink plant that is grown for the beauty of the bunched and fringed flowers and for the marvelous fragrance. This particular plant, actually a biennial, has been a favorite since my great-grandmother's day. Look for the cultivars 'Indian Carpet', 'Summer Beauty', and 'Roundabout'. These new varieties will blossom the first year if the seeds are started early. Sow seeds indoors 6 to 8 weeks before the last frost, then move seedlings to an outside cold frame when the weather has settled—they really like cool temperatures.

A perennial vine treated as an annual, **HYACINTH BEAN** *(Dolichos lablab)*, also known as the bonavista bean, the lubia bean, and the Indian bean, originated in the Old World and is considered an important food product in the tropics. These vines are rapid growers, making a run of 15 or more feet in one summer. The purple, pealike flowers are very fragrant, and after they mature they produce decorative pods about 2½ inches long with the burnished look of an antique cello. Sow seeds outdoors as soon as danger of frost has passed, spacing plants 1 foot apart. They need a trellis or strings to climb.

Hyacinth bean
(Dolichos lablab)

CHERRY PIE, or **HELIOTROPE** *(Heliotropium arborescens)*, are sweet-smelling plants from Peru. They are perennials in their native haunts but are grown as annuals in most gardens. Blooming plants bear many small violet or purple flowers, each about ¼ inch long on 15-inch plants. The scent is usually described as being sweet and fruity, on the heavy side, and plants are grown in Europe for perfume ingredients. There is also a white-flowered cultivar called 'Alba'. In order for the plants to bloom in summer, their seeds should be started by the beginning of February. You can also buy plants from the nursery center (buy only one plant and root cuttings). Heliotropes need a good, fertile soil and a spot in full sun in the North but will adapt to partial shade in the South.

Cherry pie *(Heliotropium arborescens)*

Globe candytuft *(Iberis umbellata)*

GLOBE CANDYTUFT *(Iberis umbellata)* is aptly named as it often looks good enough to eat. It is useful massed in the border, for edgings, and for cut flowers. The foot-high plants bear small, sweetly fragrant flowers in round clusters that resemble Victorian jewelry. As more flowers open, the clusters gradually become elongated, with seeds forming near the bottom of the stem. The colors vary from the traditional white with cultivars of pink, carmine, maroon, and rose now available. Sow seeds directly outdoors when the ground can be worked; for continued bloom, make successive sowings over the summer.

MOONFLOWER *(Ipomoea alba)* is a perennial vine in the tropics but grown as an annual in most gardens. This is a vine that in good summer heat can reach 10 feet by late August but 40 feet in the typical jungle. The sweet-scented flowers are pure white with a faint touch of green along the floral fold. Each flower is 6 inches wide and 6 inches long. They open in early evening like a film in slow motion, sending a very sweet, soapy fragrance into the night air. The vine flowers in 8 weeks from seed, and the developing seedpods are also unique and interesting to watch in their development.

Moonflower *(Ipomoea alba)*

Sweet peas *(Lathyrus odoratus)*

SWEET PEAS *(Lathyrus odoratus)* have been described both in poetic and garden literature for centuries. English gardens dote on their sweetly scented flowers, but to many American gardens they are strangers because of their likes and dislikes. The plants climb by tendrils, usually no higher than 6 feet, and string trellises are a perfect foil. The 2-inch flowers come in a dazzling selection of colors, including white, pink, rose, red, maroon, yellow, and many bicolor combinations. All are intensely fragrant. They bloom from late spring to summer in cooler climates, but most everywhere else they stop blooming with the heat of early summer. Soak the seeds for 24 hours in tepid water before planting. Sow outdoors as soon as the soil is above 65°F or sow indoors, using individual peat pots, as sweet peas resent any disturbance of the roots. Provide a half day of sun and use a fertile, well-drained but moist soil. They do well in pots.

BUTTER AND EGGS, also called meadow foam or poached egg flower *(Limnanthes douglasii),* is another American native annual from California. Inch-wide saucer flowers with five yellow petals edged with white appear on the foot-high plants. The scent is lightly sweet, and the blossoms are extremely popular with bees. Plants prefer cool weather and moist, but not wet, soil. Sow seeds outdoors when the soil can be worked. Plants will often self-sow.

Butter and eggs, meadow foam, or poached egg flower *(Limnanthes douglasii)*

SWEET ALYSSUM *(Lobularia maritima),* a perennial in its native home of southern Europe, is grown as an annual in most gardens. Older books call this plant *Alyssum maritumum.* The original color was white, but alyssum is now available in pink, lilac, purple, or rose. Look for 'Little Dorrit', only 4 inches high but covered with white flowers that smell lightly of sweet hay and honey. 'Rosie O'Day' bears sweetly scented rose-colored flowers. These plants are excellent as edgings along a garden pathway or tumbling over rocks in a rock garden. Sow seeds directly outside when the ground can be worked.

Sweet alyssum *(Lobularia maritima)*

Four-o'clocks
(Mirabilis jalapa)

FOUR-O'CLOCKS *(Mirabilis jalapa)* are all-time favorites for the fragrant garden: they bloom in late afternoon with fresh, brightly colored flowers about an inch wide and 2 inches long on 2- to 3-foot bushes; they bloom from early summer until frost cuts them down; and finally, their flowers have a delightful lemony sweet odor. Colors range from red to yellow, magenta, pink, crimson, white, and striped. Perennials in their native home of Peru, they are used as annuals, with seeds started about 6 weeks before the last frost and set out when all frost danger is past. The seedlings grow quickly and will overwinter outdoors except in cold climates. If you find a cultivar that is especially attractive, the tubers can be dug up and stored in winter like dahlias, then planted out the following spring.

Flowering tobacco plants have both day- and night-flowering species, including the large and stately **TOBACCO PLANT** *(Nicotiana tabacum)*, a species that will reach a height of 7 feet in the garden border. But best for the fragrant garden are the **JASMINE TOBACCO** *(N. alata)*, *N. suaveolens*, and *N. sylvestris*.

NICOTIANA ALATA is a perennial grown as an annual; it was originally imported from southern Brazil. Its flowers once opened about six p.m., but the flowers now stay open most of the day. The fragrance really explodes at night, though. Three cultivars are especially attractive: 'Grandiflora Alata' grows about 3 feet high, with large white flowers often 2 inches across; 'Lime Green', about 30 inches in height, with flowers the shade of lime sherbet; and 'Sensation Mixed' provides colors of maroon, red, white, and pink on 3-foot plants. If the plants get leggy at the end of summer, cut the mature stems back to a spot where they are enfolded by a leaf and give them a shot of liquid fertilizer; often new-flowering stems will appear.

Flowering tobacco
(Nicotiana alata)

NICOTIANA SUAVEOLENS is an annual from Australia and grows a bit short of 3 feet tall. The 2-inch-long, 1-inch-wide flowers are cream-colored, tinged with green on the outside. Rosemary Verey suggests growing it in pots so the fragrance can be enjoyed close to home.

Flowering tobacco
(Nicotiana suaveolens)

Flowering tobacco
(Nicotiana sylvestris)

NICOTIANA SYLVESTRIS, a perennial grown as an annual, is the most fragrant of the group, sending out a sweet but decidedly heavy perfume. Originally from Argentina, this plant can reach a height just short of 5 feet, especially when grown in good-quality soil.

For all the tobaccos, start seeds indoors 6 weeks before the last expected frost. Once outdoors, plants like a location in full sun (they will tolerate some shade in the Deep South) and a soil liberally laced with compost or manure. For containers use a 12-inch-diameter pot, and in the heat of summer, always water at least once a day and apply fertilizer every month.

Most **GERANIUMS** (*Pelargonium* spp.) are garden warhorses planted in pots and containers, and in public parks around the country. Most such plants bear blossoms with a bright and spicy scent, although they aren't usually considered fragrant plants. Scented geraniums, in the same genus but represented by a number of species, have small flowers, but their leaves can smell like pineapple, coconut, roses, almonds, lemons, apples, peppermints, ferns, and various citrus fruits. These leaves are often used to flavor cakes and jellies, to scent water for finger bowls at fancy luncheons, and as ingredients in potpourri.

Among the scents available, look for *Pelargonium crispum* with its lemon-scented leaves; *P. quercifolium* smells of almonds, *P. tomentosum* of peppermint, *P. graveolens* of roses, and *P. odoratissimum* of apples.

Start seeds about 10 weeks before the last frost. After the first true leaves appear, move the seedlings to individual 2-inch peat pots, then to 4-inch pots as they grow larger.

Oakleaf geranium (*Pelargonium quercifolium* 'Fair Ellen')

Petunia 'Supertunia Lavender Skies'

PETUNIAS *(Petunia x hybrida)* are often glossed over by most books dealing with fragrant flowers because many of the newer cultivars lack a strong perfume. The original plants, *Petunia axillaris* and *P. parviflora*, both imported from tropical America, were very fragrant, especially at nightfall. Today there are hundreds of cultivars, many coming true from seed and others propagated by stem cuttings. The colors vary from pure white, to pinks, reds, scarlets, blues, purples, yellow, and orange, some with picotee ruffles and some striped with color. Look for 'Blue Skies', one of the most fragrant cultivars.

If you grow petunias from seed, you will discover that only two or three plants in a dozen are delightfully fragrant. You might do better buying from a garden center, where you can smell every flat and choose those that still provide the fragrance.

MIGNONETTE *(Reseda odorata)* is never really grown for the flowers, which look very raggy and weedy, but for the sweet perfume, an odor so delightful that plants are grown commercially for an essential oil used in perfumery. Plants usually grow about 1½ feet tall with heavy stems and spatulate, limp leaves. The small flowers are yellow-green to brownish yellow, in dense racemes, and nothing to write home about. But planted by the kitchen door, or underneath a dining room window, or picked for an indoor bouquet, they are wonderful. Seedlings resent transplanting, so sow them directly outdoors as soon as the ground can be worked. Do not cover, as the seeds need light for germination. Provide some shade where the afternoon sun is hot.

Reseda lutea is much more graceful in habit than others in the genus. Billed as an annual or a biennial, plants will flower the first year from seed if started early. They bloom most of the summer on 2-foot stems that bear small light yellow flowers.

Mignonette *(Reseda odorata)*

PINCUSHION FLOWERS, or sweet scabiosa (*Scabiosa atropurpurea*), delight the gardener with sweet-smelling blossoms that are perfect 1-inch mounds of tiny blossoms, on slender stems of 2 feet or more, rising from a basal rosette of deeply divided leaves. Colors available are maroon, red, pink, rose, purple, deep purple (almost black), lavender, cream, or white. The unopened buds resemble fancy colored raspberries or little Victorian brooches. 'Dwarf Double Mixed' are fully double flowers on stems to 1½ feet. Start seeds indoors 6 weeks before the last frost and plant out to a cold frame or a protected spot in early May, as the seedlings prefer cooler weather.

Sweet scabiosa (*Scabiosa atropurpurea* 'Black Knight')

Wind poppies (*Papaver heterophyllum*)

WIND POPPIES (*Papaver heterophyllum*) are a species of native plants from California and the Baja Peninsula. Flowers have four bright brick-orange petals with a large maroon blotch at the base of each petal and many yellow stamens in the center. The scent is reminiscent of lily-of-the-valley. Stems are up to 2 feet high. They are beautiful in the rock garden or planted in a seaside garden. Sow seeds directly outdoors in spring as soon as the ground can be worked.

SCENTED MARIGOLDS or the **ANISE-FLAVORED MARIGOLD** *(Tagetes lucida)*, unlike the common marigolds that flood garden centers every spring, are really perennials originally discovered in Mexico. Plants can reach a height of 2 feet, with toothed, lance-shaped leaves and single orange-gold flowers that bloom in high summer. The whole plant is sweetly scented and leaves are used to flavor soups or dried for making herb teas. In colder climates, plants can be dug up before the hard frost and brought indoors for the winter. Indoors, sow seeds 8 weeks before the last frost and plant out in a sheltered but sunny spot after frost danger is past.

Anise-flavored marigold *(Tagetes lucida)*

Signet marigold (*Tagetes tenuifolia* 'Paprika Gem')

SIGNET MARIGOLD *(Tagetes tenuifolia)* is another surprising member of the usually smelly marigolds, being small plants—about 1 foot high—with single, 1-inch-wide flowers with yellow centers and surrounded by five yellow petals. 'Pumila' is the name applied to many dwarf and even more-compact varieties of this plant. The foliage produces the fragrance of lemon verbena; it is considered by many gardeners to be one of the most delightfully aromatic of all annuals.

Dwarf nasturtium
(Tropaeolum minus)

The **DWARF NASTURTIUM** *(Tropaeolum minus)* forms a small plant about 1 foot high, but the most popular garden subject is *T. majus*, a flower in cultivation for more than 300 years. Five-petaled and very fragrant funnel-shaped flowers, 2 inches wide and bearing a prominent spur, come in colors of deep red, mahogany, scarlet, orange, yellow, and white. The vines will grow 6 to 8 feet and are at home on a trellis, strings, or chicken-wire forms. They are also excellent in pots or containers where they can trail over the edge of a wall or just wander along the ground. Nasturtium leaves are fairly hardy, but seedlings are quickly killed by frost and do not transplant well; therefore, start seeds indoors in individual peat pots about 2 weeks before your last frost. Seeds need darkness to germinate. And, too, be wary of aphids. Nasturtiums are subject to almost overnight infestations of black aphids, so before you know it, your entire collection could be savaged. Use a pyrethrum spray (see page 179) or spray the plants with a liquid cleaner, then wash off with the fine spray of the garden hose.

NASTURTIUMS (*Tropaeolum* spp.) are typically annual plants from the cool highlands of Central and South America. The common name is from *nasus*, the Latin for *nose*, and *tortum*, Latin for *torture* or *twist*, referring to the wry face that many people make when biting into the leaves, which contain mustard oil. The leaves make great salad greens, and young seedpods are often pickled like capers.

Garden nasturtium
(Tropaeolum majus)

Two **GARDEN VERBENAS** (*Verbena* spp.) are treated as annuals. The first is 'Homestead Purple', a cultivar discovered along a Georgia roadside, its mounds of glossy green foliage producing rich purple flowers, blooming throughout the summer, and gifted with a light, sweet fragrance. The second, 'Texas Appleblossom', bears 2-inch heads of sweetly fragrant pink flowers, each with a tiny white eye. They are both excellent in pots or larger planters and do quite nicely as ground covers in full sun.

Rose verbena (*Verbena canadensis* 'Homestead Purple')

perennials

WHEN CONSIDERING FRAGRANT FLOWERS, the first reaction is to buy as many as possible. Think of going into a department store and upon reaching the perfume counter, opening every bottle and mixing the contents into one gigantic stew. The result would be unpleasant indeed. When mixing and matching fragrant flowers, the old dictum that "less is more" was never more practical.

The following plants are perennials; each has a fragrance of its own. Read the descriptions, mark those that seem to be appealing blends for the eye and the nose, then visit some of your garden friends. If you're lucky enough to live close to an arboretum that has display gardens, look at the plants in their natural surroundings. Unless noted, they are all hardy in USDA Zone 5 and south.

Valerian, Jupiter's beard, garden heliotrope *(Centranthus ruber)*

VALERIAN, JUPITER'S BEARD, or **GARDEN HELIOTROPE** *(Centranthus ruber)* is one of the dozen or so great plants for the floral border. It's a Mediterranean native, a summer bloomer, with tiny, very fragrant flowers in shades of salmon-rose, held high above gray-green foliage on 3-foot stems. Deadheading will encourage a second round of bloom. Provide well-drained, moist soil in full sun to partial shade. A white cultivar, 'Snowcloud', has an especially sweet perfume.

The **CHOCOLATE COSMOS** *(Cosmos antrosanguines)* is a fairly new perennial, and this species is the hardiest member of the clan. The cosmos-type flowers bear petals of a rich reddish brown and stand aloft on 2-foot stems, making them excellent as cut flowers. But their best feature is the marvelous fragrance of chocolate. They are not hardy in areas north of USDA Zone 7, but I suspect you could store the roots just like dahlias in colder climates.

Chocolate cosmos *(Cosmos antrosanguines)*

GARDEN, COTTAGE, or **BORDER PINKS** *(Dianthus* spp.) are a hardy tribe of mat-forming ground huggers, with gray spiky leaves and marvelous five-petaled flowers redolent with the smell of sweet cloves. The cottage pinks *(D. x allwoodii)* bear 2-inch single, semidouble, or fully double flowers, with fringed petals, often with zigzag patterns, that bloom all summer long, if properly deadheaded. Cottage pinks *(D. plumarius)* grow in tufts of gray, pointed leaves, up to 4 inches long, and produce clusters of two to five single, semidouble, or double flowers up to 1½ inch wide, with spicy fragrances like a rich talcum powder. They, too, will bloom for long periods if you shear back the spent bloom almost to nearly ground level. 'Spring Beauty' is an especially attractive cultivar. These plants are great for beds, borders, rock gardens, and in pots, where they can be moved so that their fragrance will follow you from place to place. All the pinks need a sunny spot in fast-draining, neutral to alkaline soil; if planted in acid clay they won't last long.

Cottage pinks (*D. x allwoodii* 'Pop Star')

Gas plant *(Dictamnus albus)*

The **GAS PLANT** *(Dictamnus albus)* can be a problem in the garden because it really resents being moved. But once settled in, it will live for decades. The plants, which bloom in late spring to early summer, are about 3 feet tall and produce tall stems topped with unusual-looking, fringed rosy purple flowers with five petals. The crushed leaves have a citrus odor, often mixed with the scent of anise or sweet clover. The common name refers to the age-old belief that a gas plant leaf will produce a tiny gas jet when broken, and will ignite and burn on hot, humid nights. I tried it but then was told that the seedpods rather than the leaves or the flowers produce the gas.

MEADOWSWEET *(Filipendula* spp.) are large plants, some growing to 8 feet high. They bear spectacular heads of tiny fragrant flowers, with many stamens, above strongly cut foliage. When well grown, the Manchurian meadowsweet *(F. camtschatica)* reaches a height of 10 feet and salutes the nose with massive panicles of tiny fragrant white flowers. Queen of the meadow *(F. ulmaria)* is much shorter, barely topping 6 feet, and produces 10-inch plumes of fragrant creamy white flowers. In colder gardens it's necessary to provide a winter mulch, especially in areas with frigid temperatures but little snow cover.

Meadowsweet, queen of the meadow *(Filipendula ulmaria)*

The **LEMON LILY** *(Hemerocallis lilioasphodelus)* is one of the oldest plants in American gardens, brought over from Europe in the 1600s. Blooming in late spring, it's a most desirable plant, not only for the mound of foliage but the dozens of bright yellow daylilies it will produce and the sweet fragrance each flower provides. In some colonial gardens, its lush growth banished it to a spot by the kitchen door. The daylily cultivar 'Hyperion' is another hybrid famous for its rich honeysuckle scent, present from late afternoon well into evening.

Daylily (*Hemerocallis* 'Hyperion')

Sweet rocket, dame's rocket *(Hesperis matronalis)*

SWEET ROCKETS *(Hesperis matronalis)* are short-lived perennials that have been garden delights for centuries. Dozens of ½-inch flowers, arranged in showy terminal racemes, bloom with white, purple, or lilac petals. They are wonderfully fragrant, especially in the evening. Deadhead for continued bloom and raise new plants from seed every few years as the older plants become woody and then fade away. Provide a well-drained but evenly moist soil, and in the South, partial shade, especially from noontime sun.

AUTUMN-BLOOMING HOSTA *(Hosta plantaginea)* usually blossoms from late August into September, and in colder parts of the country the blossoms are often killed by an early frost. Originally from Japan (where it was introduced from China), this is a particularly valuable garden wonder with 5-inch-long , waxy and fragrant white flowers on 8- to 10-inch stems. A new cultivar, 'Aphrodite', boasts larger blooms than on the species.

Autumn-blooming hosta *(Hosta plantaginea)*

Dwarf bearded iris *(Iris pumila)*

The **DWARF BEARDED IRIS** *(Iris pumila)* is sweet-scented upon opening. With age the aroma becomes richer and much like ripening fruit. The floral stems are from 4 to 5 inches high and topped with iris blossoms in shades of white, yellow, and purple with a number of newer cultivars that expand the color choices. The best place for this beauty is the rock garden, for the plants demand excellent drainage and a warm, sheltered spot.

Iris *(Iris graminea)*

Iris graminea bears flowers of dark purple with occasional highlights of off-white on some petals, flowering in early summer on 18-inch stems, and provides the fragrance of ripe plums.

The **ORRIS IRIS** (*Iris pallida*) has lavender-blue flowers, 4 to 5 inches wide, that have the distinct fragrance of orange blossoms and elderberry flowers. This is one of the plants grown for the production of orris, the powdered dry rhizomes that are used to make many perfumes.

Orris iris (*Iris pallida*)

Bearded iris (*Iris* x *germanica*)

Finally, the **BEARDED IRIS** (*Iris* x *germanica*), or the flag, has blue-purple falls with white beards, an amazing number of cultivars in colors from white to yellow to orange to blue. The height is between 2 and 3 feet, and plants do need a well-drained soil in a sheltered spot. The rhizomes of these irises are also a major source of orris.

Bee balm, Oswego tea (*Monarda didyma* 'Cambridge Scarlet')

BEE BALM or **OSWEGO TEA** (*Monarda didyma*) grows in upright to somewhat sprawling clumps, with 2- to 4-foot stems holding aloft tubular flowers in dense clusters. Colors range from white to pink to red, lavender, and purple. These plants prefer a sunny location in a fertile, well-drained soil and are especially attractive in wild gardens, where they are bound to invite bees, butterflies, and hummingbirds.

PHLOX (*Phlox* spp.), whether short or tall, bear tubular flowers on strong stems, many being notably fragrant. The best garden phlox are hybrids of *P. paniculata*, plants with a great range of colors, from pure white to many shades of pink and red. 'Starfire' has blossoms of bright, bright red; 'Orange Perfection' bears salmon-orange flowers on 2- to 3-foot stems. The best white was, until recently, 'Mt. Fuji', with weather-resistant mounds of delightfully fragrant flowers. A newer cultivar, 'David', provides flowers from mid-July until late September. Even if marketed as disease resistant, phlox do require extra maintenance, especially if the summer lacks rain. Water deeply at the roots during dry seasons but avoid wetting the foliage, as all of these plants are susceptible to various mildews.

Phlox (*Phlox paniculata* 'David')

PEONIES (*Paeonia* spp.) are flowers of great antiquity, the Greeks believing these splendid plants to be of divine origin. And not only are they beautiful to behold; many are extremely fragrant. The common garden or Chinese peony (*P. lactiflora*) was introduced into England in the mid-1700s and is the species that gave rise to most of the garden peonies of today. Their typical pure white flowers with golden stamens in the center are beyond description when crowded into a splendid vase and set on a table, and their fragrance will make its way around a room. Look for 'Marie Crousse' with fragrant pink flowers, the white 'Dutchesse de Nemours', the pale pink 'Sarah Bernhardt', and the species *P. delavayi*, one of the grandest plants of the tree peony family.

The catchword for growing great peonies is preparation. Before planting make sure the earth is well mixed with compost and dug deep. They also like a soil that is slightly limy rather than an acid type. Then, once they are installed, leave them alone. They will persist for decades.

Chinese peony (*Paeonia lactiflora* 'Sarah Bernhardt')

False Solomon's seal (*Maianthemum racemosum*)

FALSE SOLOMON'S SEAL (*Maianthemum racemosum*) produces 2-foot stems with terminal sprays of densely packed creamy white flowers in late spring. You can predict the fragrance by spying the dozens of small insects that flock to the stamens; they become so intoxicated they won't even know you're there. These native wildflowers want a moisture-retentive, woodland soil in light shade, especially in the South.

VIOLETS (*Viola* spp.) bear single or double 1- to 2-inch flowers of blue, lilac, violet, yellow, mauve, purple, or white. They are widely adaptable plants, often considered weedy, preferring sun to partial shade and well-drained, evenly moist humus soil. The most fragrant, and one of the best for the garden, is the sweet violet *(V. odorata)*, a species that has a long relationship with both the florist and the perfumery. When buying cultivars, remember that the larger the flower is, the weaker the fragrance will most likely be. The horned violet *(V. cornuta)*, originally from Spain and the Pyrenees and intensely fragrant, gets its name from the floral spur. Look for 'Arkwright Ruby' for maroon flowers and a great fragrance. They are not hardy above USDA Zone 6.

Horned violet (*Viola cornuta* 'Sorbet XP Morpho')

Adam's needle (*Yucca filamentosa*)

YUCCAS (*Yucca* ssp.) have been favorites in my garden ever since I found that the richly sweet, bell-like white flowers are pollinated by a tiny moth that frequents only these flowers and ignores the others. One species in particular, the Spanish dagger *(Y. glauca)*, gives the best floral show with pyramidal spires of pendant bells, 2 to 4 inches across, in clusters of hundreds. These plants need a sunny spot in well-drained soil. Once established they are drought tolerant, able to last weeks without water from the rain or from the gardener.

ROSES

I once looked up the number of references made about roses in the fourteenth (1984) edition of *Bartlett's Familiar Quotations*. The number was 267 for the singular form of the word and 134 for the plural. Quotations varied from Gertrude Stein's salute "A rose is a rose is a rose" to the song "Roses Are Blooming in Picardy" to Groucho Marx's immortal line, "Show me a rose and I'll show you the time of day." There's a reason: most civilized societies simply adore roses, both for beauty and for scent. A person standing in front of a blooming rose will almost always lean forward and sniff. Unfortunately there are a number of rose cultivars on the market today that might be big and blowsy when it comes to their blooms but painfully lacking in the scent department.

Because there are so many roses out there and so many claims to rose perfection, it's best to divide roses into categories. In each of the following category descriptions I offer suggestions for the best in fragrance.

species roses

SPECIES ROSES BEGAN THEIR GARDEN TOURS OF DUTY AS WILD ROSES collected from various places around the world. They are best described as having a genus and species name instead of a single-quoted cultivar or varietal term. Because they do come from all parts of the world, hardiness varies, and they usually bloom only once a year with fragrant single flowers of five petals. Unless noted, the following are hardy except in the most severe circumstances.

Although climbing roses must be attached to a support, once established they cover a multitude of sins. When they are close to a window, their marvelous fragrances easily brighten the room within.

Rosa carolina, or the **PASTURE ROSE,** is often found at the edges of abandoned fields, surrounded by tall grasses and wildflowers such as black-eyed Susans. Plants grow about 6 feet high and bloom in midseason with 2-inch-wide blossoms of a medium pink followed by attractive bright red hips.

Rosa carolina

Rosa foetida 'Bicolor'

Rosa foetida 'Bicolor', the so-called **AUSTRIAN COPPER ROSE,** is an early-season bloomer with petals of an orange-red on the top and yellow on the reverse. Although termed *foetida*, the smell is not all that bad, and while heavy, is like that of boxwoods. Some like it; others do not. Some gardeners think it is reminiscent of boiled linseed oil.

Rosa rugosa 'Alba'

ROSA RUGOSA is a champion of species roses. If I had my choice of only 10 plants for a fragrant garden, this rose would be one of those picked for the job. Originally found in northeastern Asia, this species has naturalized in the northeastern parts of this country. It is an excellent choice for making living fences (which will not overtake your garden). It produces large red hips, leaves that turn to attractive colors in the fall, lending a sense of architectural strength to any landscape. Marvelous mauve-pink five- to twelve-petaled blossoms go in and out of bloom for the entire season, and they are intensely fragrant.

A white form, *R. rugosa* 'Alba', is identical to the species except for pure white flowers, and another, *R. rugosa* 'Rubra', is characterized by flowers of a deep mauve-pink.

Rugosas originally came from Japan but have been so successful at naturalizing that they are often assumed to be native plants. 'Alba' bears white fragrant flowers, large and single. The *Rosa rugosa* 'Alba' reaches a height of 6 feet.

climbing roses

CLIMBING ROSES include bushes that are easily tied to trellises, and roses that ramble, naturally called rambler roses. The following are the most fragrant climbers.

Rosa 'America'

'AMERICA', a fragrant climber, is one of the few ever to win the AARS award (1976); plants reach a height of 9 to 12 feet and produce full, 4-inch double blossoms of coral-salmon.

Rosa 'New Dawn'

'NEW DAWN' was the world's first patented plant (1930). It grows to a height of 12 to 15 feet and becomes covered with fragrant light pink 3-inch blossoms of up to twenty-four petals.

'VEILCHENBLAU', originating in the early twentieth century, is often found in old gardens. The height is up to 12 feet, and the plant bears violet flowers with a white center that grow a little over 3 inches wide in mid- to late season. The flowers bear the scent of sweet green apples.

Rosa 'Veilchenblau'

SHRUB ROSES are divided into a number of classes. For purposes of the average gardener they are best described as either small, medium, or large shrubs.

'AGNES' grows about 5 feet tall and bears 3-inch light yellow double roses, with up to thirty petals, blooming in midseason and often blooming again. The flowers are very fragrant.

Rosa 'Agnes'

Rosa 'Belle Poitevine'

'BELLE POITEVINE' is a shrub up to 9 feet tall and often as wide, with up to 4-inch medium pink flowers of eighteen to twenty-four petals, and very fragrant with the decided scent of cloves.

Rosa 'Penelope'

'PENELOPE' grows between 5 and 7 feet high and bears pale, extremely fragrant coral-pink blossoms, about 3 inches across, with up to twenty-four petals.

'ROSERAIE DE L'HAŸ' is a large hybrid rugosa rose named for a famous French rose garden. Plants reach a height of 9 feet and bloom very early in the season. The dark reddish semidouble roses, over 4 inches across and with up to twenty-four petals, are very fragrant.

Rosa 'Roseraie de l'Haÿ'

old garden roses

HERE IS ANOTHER CATCHALL PHRASE that includes a number of rose types, including alba roses (descendants of a natural cross between *Rosa alba*, the white rose, and *R. canina*, the dog or briar rose); Bourbon roses (discovered on the Isle of Bourbon, now called Reunion Island); centifolia roses (from Holland); China and tea roses; damask roses (hybrids of *Rosa damascena*), gallica roses (actually grown by the Romans); and moss roses (named for the green or brown mosslike growth on both buds and stems). From the hundreds of old garden roses, I've picked the following as favorites for both color and fragrance. When you give one of these roses a spot in your fragrance garden, you are truly dealing with a piece of history.

Rosa 'Baronne Prévost'

'BARONNE PRÉVOST', a marvelous rose, goes back to 1842. Plants are about 5 feet high, bearing 4-inch double roses that can sport up to one hundred petals. Bloom is midseason with good repeat bloom in the fall.

'Rosa Mundi'

'ROSA MUNDI' has been known since before 1581. It's a striped sort of *Rosa gallica officinalis*, the apothecary rose or the red rose of Lancaster, and named for Fair Rosamund, the mistress of King Henry II of England. There are no two ways about it: this is a beautiful rose, and in fact is the earliest and most beautiful of all the striped roses. No two blossoms are marked in the same way. Sweetly fragrant flowers open in midseason, are up to 3½ inches wide with eighteen to twenty-four petals, eventually opening to surround a mass of golden stamens. Round red rose hips appear later in the summer.

hybrid tea roses

THESE ARE THE ROSES THAT PEOPLE USUALLY IMAGINE WHEN THINKING OF ROSES. They are the most popular of all, great for cutting, and many will happily grow in tubs and containers. Unfortunately, fragrance has often been traded in for size of bloom. However, a few still can be grown for their exceptional perfume. Look for the following roses, which, unless noted, are also disease resistant and winter hardy.

Whether small or large, a rose garden of mixed colors and mixed fragrances not only charms the landscape but provides cut flowers for an elegant dining table—not to mention an occasional corsage.

'KAISERIN AUGUSTE VIKTORIA' is one of the oldest hybrid teas (it was introduced in 1891) still in cultivation. The 4-inch-wide flowers are creamy white and full of petals (usually more than one hundred), are fairly constant with repeat blooms, and are very fragrant.

Rosa 'Kaiserin Auguste Viktoria'

Rosa 'Medallion'

'MEDALLION', a 1973 AARS winner, is a classic rose that likes cool weather; as a cut flower, it enjoys a very long vase life. The light apricot flowers are more than 5 inches across, with up to thirty-five petals. It blooms in midseason and often repeats. The fragrance is rich and fruity. In cold climates, it needs good winter protection, including heavy mulching.

Rosa 'Peace'

While the **'PEACE'** rose is often called the rose of the century, a winner of many awards in the U.S. and abroad, it has only a slight fragrance. 'Pink Peace', however, is something else again. Here is a blossom up to 6 inches across, with more than fifty petals of medium to deep pink riding on top of 5-foot vigorous and bushy plants. It is a very fragrant rose.

'TROPICANA' was another AARS Award–winner and the first pure rose of fluorescent orange. It is often described as the third-greatest-selling rose in this century. Blossoms are 5 inches across with thirty to thirty-five petals of bright orange; they have a rich and fruity scent.

Rosa 'Tropicana'

Among the diseases waiting in the wings are powdery mildew, that dusty fungal growth that runs rampant during hot, humid weather. Remove badly infected leaves, try to increase air circulation, and check with your garden center for a sulfur-based dusting powder.

Virus attacks turn healthy leaves into something deformed and stunted. Remove and destroy infected plants, make sure that your shears are sharp and clean, and buy healthy plants from reputable sources.

Rust is a fungus that causes powdery orange spots on the undersides of leaves. Remove and destroy infected leaves and check for a suitable dusting powder at the garden center.

Aphids are soft little green or brown insects that suck the life out of plants. Wash them off with a powerful spray of water from the hose. If this doesn't work, try one of the liquid cleaners like Fantastik or an insecticidal soap.

Japanese beetles love rose foliage. Use traps to collect, then destroy.

Spider mites are tiny red, brown, or golden relatives of spiders that form on the undersides of leaves, spin many tiny webs, suck the life out of the leaf, then breed like mad, eventually unleashing millions of pests in your garden. Spray the bottom of the leaves with a hard spray of water from the hose and keep it up daily for at least 2 weeks.

choices available. I have left out a few of the common fragrant bulbs like hyacinths and paper-white narcissus in order to mention the more unusual ones.

Lily-of-the-valley (*Convallaria majalis*)

LILY-OF-THE-VALLEY *(Convallaria majalis)* are actually not bulbs but pips, but like roses, by any other name they would smell as sweet. These charmers can be used in beds, borders, rock gardens, and as ground covers. They make lovely cut flowers, not to mention their importance as a perfumery plant. Brought over by colonists, they have been in America since the 1600s and used as ground covers in cemeteries. The sprays of tiny nodding bells appear in late spring or early summer and can be forced into early bloom in a window garden by potting pips in the fall and keeping them cold for 8 to 12 weeks. There are double forms, which I think of as unnecessary, and a form with pink flowers that, while different, is rather pleasant in the garden. It should be noted that in such a delightful plant the berries and the rootstocks are poisonous. Lily-of-the-valley are cold hardy from Zone 4 south but do not like areas with very warm weather, like the Deep South.

FREESIAS (*Freesia* spp.) are members of the iris family and hail from South Africa. I was introduced to these intensely fragrant flowers one bleak day in March, when a local florist showed me pots of very tall leaves—all tied up with string—that surrounded sprays of nodding waxy yellow flowers. They are easy to grow in containers (or outdoors in Zone 9 and south) by planting six precooled corms to a pot, watering well, then leaving them alone for 10 days. As the leaves develop, stake them to prevent their flopping over. The Dutch now supply precooled bulbs for planting outdoors in the summertime, too.

Freesia (*Freesia* spp.)

Madonna lily (*Lilium candidum*)

The **GARDEN LILIES** (*Lilium* spp.) represent a large genus of bulbous plants that are relatively easy to grow, both in the garden or, if space is limited, in pots. The majority of blossoms produce a rich and marvelous scent. Madonna lilies (*Lilium candidum*) have flourished in gardens since the days of the Minoan culture, fifteen hundred years before the birth of Christ. Medieval gardens had whole corners dedicated to these symbols of purity. The immaculate white and fragrant flowers perch on top of stems that may grow up to 6 feet tall, with up to fifteen flowers per stem. Unlike other lilies, these plants need only an inch or two of soil over the top of the bulb. They should be heavily mulched in areas with very cold winters but little snow cover.

Last summer on a rainy afternoon, I went out to check a large clump of the **GOLD-BANDED LILY** *(Lilium auratum)* blooming at the edge of my fern garden. Not only were they fragrant, but the heady smell could be detected from 15 feet away.

Lily *(Lilium auratum var auratum)*

Formosa lily *(Lilium formosanum)*

For late-summer bloom, try the **FORMOSA LILY**, *Lilium formosanum*, with its elegant, 6-inch-long white blossoms that bloom on 4- to 6-foot stems.

The most important thing to remember about lilies is that, unlike other bulbs, they are never dormant and the scales that surround the bulb have no protective covering and are easily broken. Handle them with care when planting. A few species, like the Madonna lily, want shallow planting, but most of the other species and cultivars have flowering stems that produce roots as they grow up to the surface; set them 4 to 8 inches deep. If your soil is heavy, dig the hole a bit deeper and put some sand at the bottom, then place a teaspoon of bonemeal in the bottom of each hole. After inserting the bulb, add about an inch more sand before covering it with soil.

The **TUBEROSE** *(Polianthes tuberosa)* was once one of the most popular fragrant plants in the civilized world. Unfortunately, because it became popular as a funeral parlor flower, it fell out of public favor. Today, of course, we can forget the past and again plant a few bulbs in the summer border or in pots for the terrace, and the marvelous sweet scent will again delight the senses. There are two varieties: 'Mexican Everblooming', which reaches a height of 4 feet and bears 2-inch-long waxy, extremely fragrant white flowers, and 'The Pearl', which is 16 inches high and bears 2-inch double flowers. The bulblike bases are really rhizomes, as these plants are in the same family as yuccas and agaves. Unless you live in an area where the ground doesn't freeze (Zone 9), store the roots in a warm dry place during the winter. Tuberoses can be forced for November bloom.

Tuberose *(Polianthes tuberosa)*

Summer hyacinth *(Galtonia candicans)*

The **SUMMER HYACINTH** *(Galtonia candicans)* struggles in the truly cold parts of the country, but in USDA Zone 6 and warmer, it does beautifully. You do not have to dig them up in Zone 6. Forty-inch stems bear twenty to thirty fragrant bell-shaped flowers of white with a touch of green at the base. The individual flowers look like spring hyacinths, but are, to my mind, far more attractive. If snow cover is scarce in your garden and you don't have time to mulch heavily, plant the bulbs in mesh bags and dig them up for storage in the winter. It's worth the effort.

SPECIES TULIPS (*Tulipa* spp.) are little-known bulbs often outstepped, but not outclassed, by their bigger relatives, the cottage and Darwin tulips, those bright and blowzy blossoms so loved by spring flower devotees. Species tulips are perfect for edges of the wild garden, for the rock garden, between paving stones, and in pots. They want full sun, well-drained soil, and summer heat.

Wild tulip (*Tulipa sylvestris*)

The following are three of the most fragrant species. In Iran and Syria, *T. aucheriana* is found on rugged mountain slopes, producing one to three scented flowers from each tiny bulb. The star-shaped flowers open flat on 4-inch stems, and each pink petal has a yellow blotch at the base. From Asia Minor comes *T. batalinii*, available in a number of cultivars, including the most beautiful 'Red Jewel', 'Yellow Jewel', and 'Bronze Charm'. The latter variety adds a glowing bronze hue to the early-spring garden. Another fragrant beauty is *T. celsiana persica*, naturalized in Spain, France, and Morocco, with petals of a clear yellow and outer petals lightly tinged with bronze. Finally, *T. sylvestris* hails from West Africa and southern Europe and produces many yellow flowers, pendent in bud but standing upright in bloom. Because they are sweetly scented, they should be planted at the edge of a path or along the top of a garden wall.

It should be noted that unscrupulous bulb companies still gather these bulbs from the wild. So buy them only from catalogs that stipulate the bulbs are propagated at the nursery.

shrubs and small trees

THE FOLLOWING SHRUBS AND SMALL TREES have been chosen to combine fragrant flowers, good form, and small stature. As such, they are well suited for the typical backyard. The vines are all reasonably well behaved, except for the Oriental wisterias; the dangers of growing these fragrant beauties is well documented below.

WHITE FORSYTHIA *(Abeliophyllum distichum)*, a 1924 shrub introduction, was first imported from central Korea. Searching for a popular name, some nurseryman decided on the white forsythia, a term that certainly describes the flowers but is botanically incorrect. However, this shrub is a prize addition to any garden no matter what you call it. The lovely white flowers are heavily fragrant, opening in early spring. If cut earlier in the season, they can be forced for indoor bloom. After flowering, the shrub becomes an excellent backdrop for other garden perennials. Flower buds appear in late summer, so prune in the spring after blossoming is over for the year. Provide ordinary garden soil. This beauty is hardy from Zones 5 to 8. It does not do well in areas where the summers are exceptionally warm.

White forsythia *(Abeliophyllum distichum)*

Butterfly bush (*Buddleia davidii* 'Black Knight')

BUTTERFLY BUSH (*Buddleia* spp.) has a lilaclike fragrance. If you garden in Zone 5, butterfly bushes die back every winter, only to burst forth in the spring; in the South, they should be cut back to the stature of a short bush. By summer, they produce florific racemes of fragrant little flowers. Happily, these bushes are not fussy as to soil. However, like most plants, they do appreciate good drainage, and while liking full sun, they will adapt to partial shade, especially in the South.

CAROLINA ALLSPICE (*Calycanthus floridus*) bears somewhat strange, reddish brown leathery-petaled flowers that open flat and are extremely fragrant. They are deciduous, losing leaves in the winter, but are quite beautiful in the formal or wild garden. Be sure to keep them close to any garden path so that you can enjoy their scent. Height varies between 4 and 10 feet, and they can be pruned in late winter or early spring to keep them within bounds. Soil should be well drained and evenly moist. The allspice prefers full sun in the North and woodland conditions in the South.

Carolina allspice (*Calycanthus floridus*)

Fringe tree (*Chionanthus virginicus*)

FRINGE TREES (*Chionanthus virginicus*) are one of my garden favorites. According to location, they could be termed large shrubs or small trees, eventually reaching 20 feet in height and width but easily kept within bounds with pruning. The fringelike white flowers bloom in spring; they are four-petaled in 6-inch clusters. They send out a sweet fragrance, especially through shaded woodland gardens. Blue berries appear in the fall. In the garden next door, Doan Ogden wanted a Japanese look to his garden, so he weighted down a fringe tree with ropes and concrete blocks until it stayed in a bent position; it now frames the entrance to his moss garden. Fringe trees are hardy from USDA Zones 5 to 8.

Variegated winter daphne (*Daphne odora* 'Maejima')

The **DAPHNES** (*Daphne* spp.) are small, deciduous evergreen shrubs that bloom with ½-inch flowers packed into terminal heads. The flowers come in a variety of colors that range from white to pink to purple. Many species are intensely fragrant. These shrubs prefer sun to partial shade in the Deep South and they like humusy, well-drained soil that's on the slightly moist side. They are perfect as small specimen plants, in borders, in rock gardens, and in containers.

My favorite is the **WINTER DAPHNE** (*Daphne odora*), a shrub that blooms in late winter and reaches a height of 3 to 4 feet with a 3-foot spread. The blooms are very fragrant, rosy purple without and white within. 'Variegata' has leaves edged with dashes of a creamy white tint. They are slow to establish themselves and resent areas with a hard winter.

Sweetspire *(Itea virginica)*

SWEETSPIRE *(Itea virginica)* are shrubs or small trees, between 8 and 16 feet in height, again according to location and pruning. The tiny fragrant white flowers in drooping foot-long clusters bloom in late spring or early summer. This is a marvelous plant for the back of the border so that the scent can drift over the garden's edge and be available to passersby. Soil should be well drained and evenly moist. They are hardy from USDA Zones 5 to 9.

OREGON GRAPES *(Mahonia* spp.) are broad-leaved evergreen shrubs that look like hollies but are really members of the barberry family. They range in height from 3 to 10 feet and usually bloom in late winter to early summer with fragrant 3- to 6-inch drooping racemes of small buttery yellow, waxy-petaled blossoms. These are followed in the fall by purplish black fruits, rather like small, pointed grapes, that last through the winter if your bird population doesn't find them. Bushes are hardy from USDA Zones 6 to 9. They prefer a well-drained, evenly moist, acidic garden soil. Cut them back after flowering, and even old bushes will send up new growth. The Japanese mahonia *(M. japonica)* is a recommended species, but *M. aquifolium* and *M. bealei* are both excellent additions to the garden.

Oregon grape *(Mahonia aquifolium)*

Sweet mock orange
(Philadelphus coronarius)

MOCK ORANGES *(Philadelphus* spp.), old-fashioned deciduous shrubs from 4 to 12 feet in height, are known for their extremely fragrant white flowers. A good shrub may become so loaded with white cup-shaped flowers that its branches will bend under the weight. Sweet mock orange *(P. coronarius)* has very fragrant flowers and is represented by a number of cultivars, hardy from Zone 5 and south; some grow to 10 feet and others are quite short. A hybrid between *P. coronarius* and *P. microphyllus* produced the cultivar 'Avalanche', bearing white flowers that are exceptionally rich and sweet. Provide well-drained soil and a spot in full sun in the North and partial shade in the South. Thin out overcrowded shoots after flowers fade, but be careful of young shoots as they bear flowers the following year.

LILACS *(Syringa vulgaris)* arrived in America in the middle 1600s. The word is old, taken from the Arabic *laylak* and the Persian *nilak*, this last from *nil*, meaning blue. By 1960, there were about six hundred known cultivars produced in seven distinct colors: white (including cream), violet, lilac, blue, pink, purple, and red. There are also single and double flowers. "When lilacs last in the dooryard bloomed," Walt Whitman wrote in the mid-1800s. The flowers are lovely, the fragrance quite wonderful. Among the more attractive cultivars are 'Ellen Willmott', bearing double white flowers; 'Belle de Nancy', with flowers of double pink; and for those with limited space, *S. patula* 'Miss Kim', a Korean lilac of small stature (5 by 5 feet when mature).

Lilacs need a reasonably fertile, well-drained soil, preferably with a good organic content. Lilacs should be deadheaded to save energy and also for cosmetic reasons. If an old bush is cut way back, it may be 3 years before new flowering begins.

Manchurian lilac (*Syringa pubescens* subsp. *patula* 'Miss Kim')

vines

THE VINES LISTED BELOW all have very fragrant flowers, and except for the Oriental wisterias, can be kept within bounds merely by selective pruning.

Sweet autumn clematis
(*Clematis* terniflora)

Except for the bush varieties *(Clematis heracleifolia)*, **CLEMATISES** are vining or semi-woody climbers. A number are fragrant, but three special species immediately spring to mind. All clematises like a slightly sweet soil, so when you plant, add a bit of limestone to the soil. In the North they appreciate full sun, but in the South some shade. It should be noted that all clematises like a cool root run: the vines might prefer the light, but the base of the plant where it enters the earth appreciates a shady, slightly moist spot.

The **WINTER-BLOOMING CLEMATIS** *(Clematis armandii)* is very special because it blooms in midwinter and also because its evergreen foliage is beautiful without the flowers. Unfortunately, it is not hardy north of USDA Zone 7, and even there it can suffer if subjected to chill and below-zero winds.

The **SWEET AUTUMN CLEMATIS** *(Clematis terniflora)* blooms in early fall with hundreds of small, sweet-smelling white blossoms. This vine is especially magnificent when allowed to climb its way to the top of evergreen trees, to which it does no harm. Zone 5.

CLEMATIS HERACLEIFOLIA DAVIDIANA is a bush-forming showy species that blooms with dense clusters of deep blue fragrant flowers on 4-foot stems.

CAROLINA JESSAMINE *(Gelsemium sempervirens)* is an evergreen vine that needs warm winters to survive (it's only reliably hardy from Zone 7 south). From late winter to early spring, a mature vine is covered with hundreds of tubular, fragrant sunshine yellow blossoms that are especially noticeable when growing in the wild along the wooded edges of the interstates. This vine is easily grown against trellises, on fences, or naturalized. Gardeners in areas of Zone 6 and below can grow it in containers.

Carolina jessamine (*Gelsemium sempervirens* 'Margarita')

Goldflame honeysuckle (*Lonicera x heckrottii* 'Goldflame')

The **HONEYSUCKLES** (*Lonicera* spp.) are shrubs or vines known for their honey-sweet flowers. Among the most fragrant vines are *L. japónica* and *L.* 'Halliana'. Unfortunately, they are also the most invasive, with the ability to reach over 30 feet, depending on the climate. If you have the space (and the strength) for this vine, allow it to scamper up a dead tree trunk or twine around a stout trellis. And nothing is better to carpet a difficult bank or a bare slope that has resisted everything you've planted. But be warned—they won't remain only where you want them. The vines bloom from late spring into summer.

Wisteria (*Wisteria sinensis*)

There is a danger when recommending the **WISTERIA** (*Wisteria* spp.) clan for the fragrant garden. After all, next to kudzu and honeysuckle, these marching vines will quickly take over most provided trellises and arbors, then set their sights for far horizons. The strength of these grasping vines can actually bend iron pipes. However, if you are fortunate enough to sit beneath a wisteria bower when it's in bloom, you'll never forget the experience.

Wisteria floribunda is the Japanese species with a number of cultivars now available. 'Ivory Towers' has long racemes of pure white blossoms.

Wisteria sinensis, the Chinese wisteria, blooms before the foliage appears.

Wisteria venusta is our American species and unlike its Asian relatives, completely harmless in the garden.

Because of the meandering habits of wisterias, it's best to grow this vine under the watchful eye of volunteers who will promise to trim every tendril as it advances toward other trees and houses. You may want to grow them in containers, where the control is far greater and the vines can be trimmed as a small tree or kept to one trellis. Provide full sun except in the Deep South, where some afternoon shade is appreciated. They are not fussy as to soil type, but they do want good drainage. If your vine doesn't produce flowers, it's either due to a rooted cutting, which will never flower, or to an excess of nitrogen. For the first problem check your supplier; for the second, use a 0-10-10 formula during the growing season.

houseplants

NOT EVERYBODY HAS A BACKYARD SUITED TO GARDENING, nor do we all want to spend the time and energy necessary to provide and maintain an outdoor garden. For those gardeners with limited space or time, the following plants are especially suited for the indoor environment, doing well in pots and in the lower light levels found in most homes, even those with very clean windows.

Arabian coffee plant
(Coffea arabica)

The **ARABIAN COFFEE PLANT** *(Coffea arabica)* is the major source of commercial coffee and the principal coffee-producing species grown in Latin America. But you can have your own Juan Valdez favorite in your garden room or sunporch as long as you keep the temperatures above 55°F and have plenty of bright light. In containers, coffee grows up to 5 or 6 feet, but with good environmental care can grow as tall as 10 feet. Branches are decked with shiny green leaves. In late spring and early summer, clusters of fragrant white starry flowers actually produce pulpy red berries, each containing the two seeds or "beans" that are roasted for coffee. The fruits do take several months to ripen. Keep soil evenly moist and set the plant in filtered sun.

Gardenia (*Gardenia jasminoides*)

The **CAPE JASMINE** is a gardenia (*Gardenia jasminoides*) of great beauty with a fragrance to match. The cultivar 'Prostrata', a dwarf variety, has shiny leaves, a compact growth habit, and small waxy-petaled gardenias throughout the year, peaking from spring into summer. Provide full sun in winter, partial sun in summer, and a minimum temperature of 60°F.

WAX PLANTS (*Hoya* spp.) have been houseplant favorites since the Victorian era. They are exceptional when grown in pots and have a great tolerance to gardeners who ignore them for weeks on end. The most popular members of the clan are *H. carnosa* and *H. bella*. When they bloom, clusters of 12 to 15 perfect star-shaped flowers, each more fragrant than the next and each on a slim stem, open like a living fireworks display. The blossoms look as though they were carved from wax. Then, too, almost every flower will produce a crystal drop of nectar that is incredibly sweet. The smell of warm mocha java is produced by *H. coronaria; H. odorata* smells of citrus in general and lemons in particular; *H. polyneura*, or the fishtail hoya, produces fragrant gems of pure white, each flower boasting a blush-pink center. They prefer a good houseplant soil, evenly moist, but will survive a lack of water for weeks. A great pot is a wire-mesh basket; line it with a sheet of sphagnum moss.

Wax plant (*Hoya carnosa*)

Winter jasmine (*Jasminum polyanthum*)

WINTER JASMINE (*Jasminum polyanthum*) usually provides its masses of fragrant snow-white flowers in the dead of winter. This is a great basket plant, keeping to a height and width of about 3 feet in a container. The minimum temperature is 35°F, with 60°F the average, but to bloom, there has to be a spell of days with temperatures below 60°F.

JASMINUM MOLLE hails from Australia, producing sweetly scented flowers in late summer and fall. When grown in containers, the vines reach lengths of 3 feet and need a minimum temperature of 50°F.

POET'S JASMINE (*Jasminum officinale grandiflorum*), sometimes called French perfume jasmine, has fragrant double white flowers that halt their display only during late winter. In containers, the general length of the vines remains within the 3-foot range. Provide full sun and a minimum temperature of 45°F.

JASMINUM SAMBAC, 'Grand Duke of Tuscany', produces thick, fully double white blooms on the stem tips. Unlike the jasmine vines, this is a bush type. In Southeast Asia, a perfumed drink is made by soaking the flowers overnight in water. Provide full sun and minimum temperatures of 60°F.

Orange jasmine *(Murraya paniculata)*

In bloom, **ORANGE JASMINE** *(Murraya paniculata)* produces the scent of orange blossoms, usually throughout the year; when the plant isn't in bloom, it's in bud. Provide full sun and a minimum temperature of 45°F.

MADAGASCAR JASMINE *(Stephanotis floribunda)* is a tropical climber with thick, leathery, glossy dark green leaves on stems that bloom in the winter months, producing clusters of lovely waxy, trumpet-shaped white flowers that flare out to five pointed lobes. This is another flower often used for wedding bouquets. Provide full sun and keep the minimum temperature around 60°F. The vines bloom in spring and summer.

Madagascar jasmine *(Stephanotis floribunda)*

Known as the **CONFEDERATE JASMINE** (for the Confederate States of Malaysia), *Trachelospermum jasminoides* bears fragrant white star-shaped blooms in early spring.

Confederate jasmine
(Trachelospermum jasminoides)

Fragrant snowball
(Viburnum x carcephalum)

The **FRAGRANT SNOWBALL** *(Viburnum x carcephalum)* bears large clusters of sweetly fragrant blossoms that are often as wide as 6 inches across.

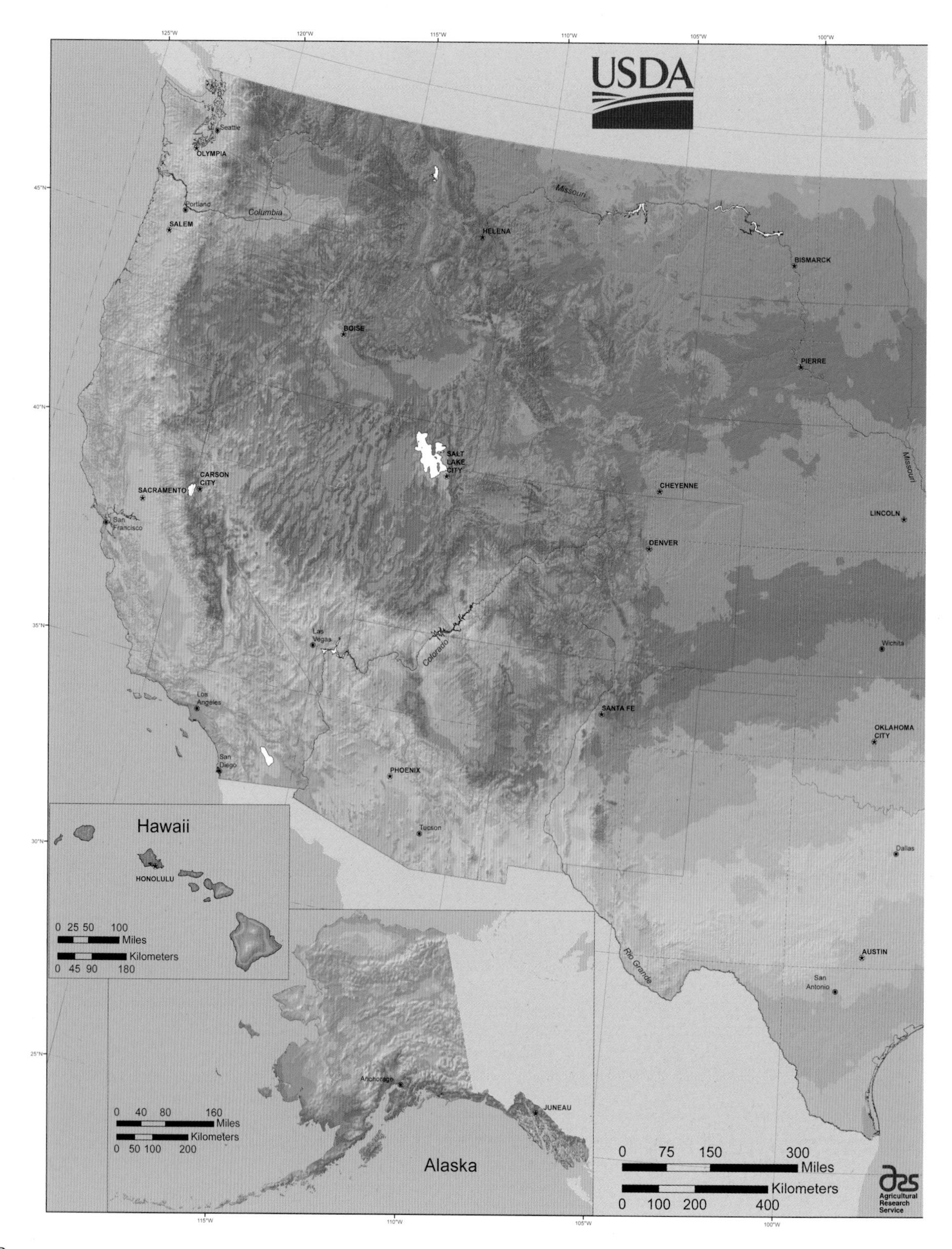

USDA
Seattle
OLYMPIA
Portland
Columbia
SALEM
Missouri
HELENA
BISMARCK
BOISE
PIERRE
SALT
LAKE
CITY
CARSON
CITY
SACRAMENTO
San
Francisco
CHEYENNE
Missouri
LINCOLN
DENVER
Las
Vegas
Colorado
Wichita
Los
Angeles
SANTA FE
OKLAHOMA
CITY
San
Diego
PHOENIX
Hawaii
HONOLULU
Tucson
Dallas
0 25 50 100
Miles
Kilometers
0 45 90 180
Rio Grande
AUSTIN
San
Antonio
Anchorage
JUNEAU
0 40 80 160
Miles
Kilometers
0 50 100 200
Alaska
0 75 150 300
Miles
Kilometers
0 100 200 400
Agricultural
Research
Service

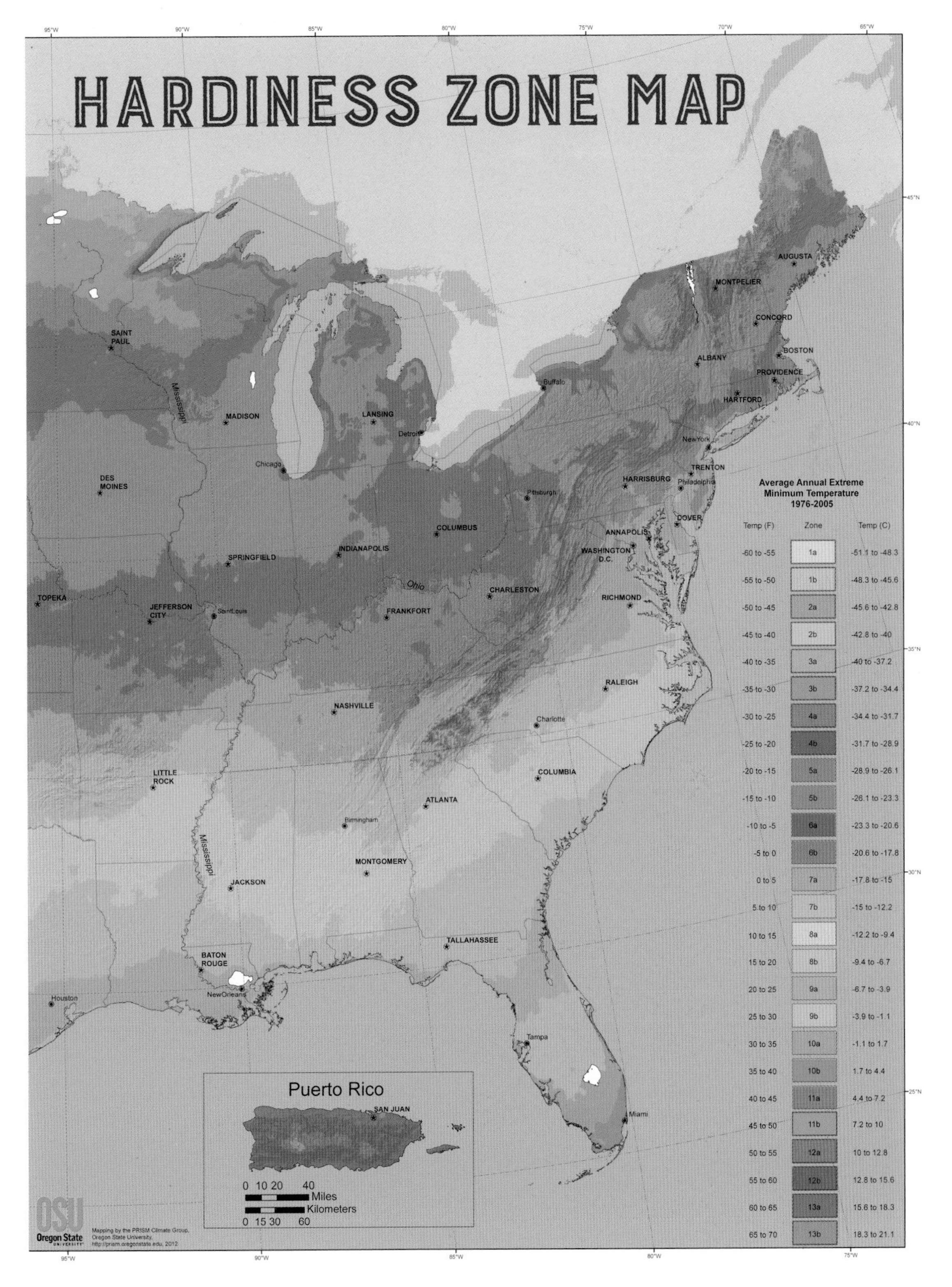

HARDINESS ZONE MAP
AUGUSTA
MONTPELIER
CONCORD
BOSTON
ALBANY
PROVIDENCE
HARTFORD
Buffalo
SAINT PAUL
Mississippi
MADISON
LANSING
Detroit
New York
TRENTON
Chicago
HARRISBURG
Philadelphia
DES MOINES
Pittsburgh
DOVER
COLUMBUS
ANNAPOLIS
WASHINGTON D.C.
INDIANAPOLIS
SPRINGFIELD
Ohio
CHARLESTON
RICHMOND
TOPEKA
JEFFERSON CITY
Saint Louis
FRANKFORT
RALEIGH
NASHVILLE
Charlotte
LITTLE ROCK
COLUMBIA
ATLANTA
Birmingham
Mississippi
MONTGOMERY
JACKSON
TALLAHASSEE
BATON ROUGE
New Orleans
Houston
Tampa
Miami
Puerto Rico
SAN JUAN
0 10 20 40 Miles
0 15 30 60 Kilometers
OSU
Oregon State University
Mapping by the PRISM Climate Group, Oregon State University, http://prism.oregonstate.edu, 2012
Average Annual Extreme Minimum Temperature 1976-2005
Temp (F) | Zone | Temp (C)
-60 to -55 | 1a | -51.1 to -48.3
-55 to -50 | 1b | -48.3 to -45.6
-50 to -45 | 2a | -45.6 to -42.8
-45 to -40 | 2b | -42.8 to -40
-40 to -35 | 3a | -40 to -37.2
-35 to -30 | 3b | -37.2 to -34.4
-30 to -25 | 4a | -34.4 to -31.7
-25 to -20 | 4b | -31.7 to -28.9
-20 to -15 | 5a | -28.9 to -26.1
-15 to -10 | 5b | -26.1 to -23.3
-10 to -5 | 6a | -23.3 to -20.6
-5 to 0 | 6b | -20.6 to -17.8
0 to 5 | 7a | -17.8 to -15
5 to 10 | 7b | -15 to -12.2
10 to 15 | 8a | -12.2 to -9.4
15 to 20 | 8b | -9.4 to -6.7
20 to 25 | 9a | -6.7 to -3.9
25 to 30 | 9b | -3.9 to -1.1
30 to 35 | 10a | -1.1 to 1.7
35 to 40 | 10b | 1.7 to 4.4
40 to 45 | 11a | 4.4 to 7.2
45 to 50 | 11b | 7.2 to 10
50 to 55 | 12a | 10 to 12.8
55 to 60 | 12b | 12.8 to 15.6
60 to 65 | 13a | 15.6 to 18.3
65 to 70 | 13b | 18.3 to 21.1

PHOTOGRAPHY CREDITS

Trudy Broussard: 171

Sue Brown: 174 (all), 177 (top), 181 (top), 191 (top)

Janet Davis: ii, iv, vi, 4 (top), 17 (all), 21, 23, 29, 31, 32, 33, 34, 39, 41, 42, 43, 44, 48, 50, 56, 57, 58, 63, 68, 69, 70, 79, 81, 83, 86, 87, 90, 92, 93, 95, 104, 107, 115, 117, 118, 120, 136 (all), 144, 145 (bottom), 146 (top), 149 (all), 150 (bottom), 151 (all), 152, 153 (all), 154 (all), 155 (bottom), 156 (bottom), 158, 159 (all), 161 (all), 162 (middle), 162 (bottom), 163 (top), 164 (all), 165 (bottom), 166 (top), 169 (all), 172 (bottom), 173 (all), 175 (all), 177 (bottom), 181 (bottom), 182 (all), 183 (all), 184, 186 (all), 187 (top), 189 (top), 190, 192, 194 (bottom), 195, 196 (top), 197 (all)

Janet Davis, designed by Bev Koffel: 13 (bottom)

Janet Davis, at the Center for Urban Horticulture: 40

Janet Davis, designed by Janet Draper: 9 (top), 72

Janet Davis, designed by Nancy Goldman: 9 (bottom), 202

Janet Davis, designed by Marnie Wright: 15, 143

Janet Davis, designed by Paul Zammit: 10, 11 (all), 37, 67, 131

Janet Davis, designed by Paul Zammit at the Toronto Botanical Garden: 22

Lynn Hunt: 13 (top), 14, 28, 46, 59, 64, 74, 91, 96, 148 (top), 168, 172 (top), 176

Betty Mackey: 38, 66, 100

Nancy J. Ondra: i, vii, 2, 4 (bottom), 5, 6, 8, 12, 13 (middle), 16, 18, 19, 20, 24, 25, 26, 27, 30, 35, 36, 45, 47, 49, 51, 52, 53, 54, 55, 60, 61, 62, 65, 71, 73, 75, 76, 78, 80, 82, 84, 85, 88, 89, 94, 97, 98, 99, 101, 102, 103, 105, 106, 108, 109, 110, 111, 112, 113, 114, 116, 119,121, 122, 123, 125, 127, 129, 130, 134, 137, 140, 141, 145 (top), 146 (bottom), 147 (bottom), 148 (bottom), 150 (top), 156 (top), 157, 160 (all), 162 (top), 163 (bottom), 166 (bottom), 170, 178 (bottom), 188 (all), 191 (bottom), 196 (bottom), 200

PhilipC57/Shutterstock.com: 178 (top)

DoreenWynja.com Photography: 138, 147 (top), 155 (top), 180, 185, 187 (bottom), 193

DoreenWynja.com for Monrovia: 77, 132, 165 (top), 189 (bottom), 194 (top)

COVER:

Background photo © fotohunter/Shutterstock.com

Photos on left, from top to bottom: © Janet Davis, © Nancy J. Ondra, © Nancy J. Ondra, © Nancy J. Ondra

4
5
2

INDEX

A

B

D

E

F

G

H

I

J

L

M

O

P

Q

R

U

W

Z